# Switze

# Travel Guide

# for 2023, 2024,

# and Beyond

A Guidebook to

this Beautiful Country

Alexander Harris

© **Copyright 2023 - All rights reserved.**

The content contained within this book may not be reproduced, duplicated or transmitted without direct written permission from the author or the publisher.

Under no circumstances will any blame or legal responsibility be held against the publisher, or author, for any damages, reparation, or monetary loss due to the information contained within this book, either directly or indirectly.

## Legal Notice:

This book is copyright protected. It is only for personal use. You cannot amend, distribute, sell, use, quote or paraphrase any part, or the content within this book, without the consent of the author or publisher.

## Disclaimer Notice:

Please note the information contained within this document is for educational and entertainment purposes only. All effort has been executed to present accurate, up to date, reliable, complete information. No warranties of any kind are declared or implied. Readers acknowledge that the author is not engaging in the rendering of legal, financial, medical or professional advice. The content within this book has been derived from various sources. Please consult a licensed professional before attempting any techniques outlined in this book.

By reading this document, the reader agrees that under no circumstances is the author responsible for any losses, direct or indirect, that are incurred as a result of the use of information contained within this document, including, but not limited to, errors, omissions, or inaccuracies.

# Table of Contents

## The Swiss Alps .......... 1
Facts about the Mountains .......... 1
Facts about the Glaciers .......... 2
Facts about the Hiking Trails .......... 3
Facts about Switzerland's Primary Rivers .......... 4

## The Swiss Plateau .......... 9
Switzerland's Most-Produced Agriculture Commodities .......... 10

## The Swiss Jura .......... 14
The Jura Crest Trail .......... 16

## Switzerland Culture .......... 18
Swiss National Museum .......... 20
Kunstmuseum Basel .......... 21
Lucerne Transportation Museum .......... 22
The Olympic Museum .......... 23
Red Cross and Red Crescent International Museum 25

## Swiss Cuisine .......... 27
Other Traditional Swiss Foods Worth Trying .......... 29
Switzerland's Best Restaurants - Top 10 .......... 32
    Vieux Chalet (Best for Raclette) .......... 32
    Le Chalet de Gruyères (Best for Fondue) .......... 33

Zeughauskeller (Best for Hearty Swiss Fare) ........ 33

Tea Room Frutal (Best for Desserts) ..................... 34

Brasserie Lipp (Best for Classic French Cuisine) . 35

Findlerhof (Best Dining with a View) .................... 36

Haus Hiltl, Zurich (Best Vegetarian Dining) ........ 36

The Restaurant at the Chedi (Best International Dining) .................................................................... 37

## Switzerland's Climate ............................................... 39

## Best Luxurious Hotels in Switzerland .................... 42

1. Badrutt's Palace Hotel ................................. 42

2. The Dolder Grand ....................................... 43

3. The Woodward ............................................ 44

4. Beau-Rivage Palace ..................................... 46

5. The Chedi Andermatt ................................. 47

6. Gstaad Palace .............................................. 48

7. Kulm Hotel .................................................. 49

8. Grand Hotel Kronenhof Pontresina ........... 50

9. The Omnia ................................................... 52

10. Grand Hotel Les Trois Rois ....................... 53

## Seasonal Outdoor Activities to Enjoy in Switzerland ...................................................................................... 55

-Spring- ............................................................ 55

-Summer- ......................................................... 56

-Autumn- ................................................................ 59

-Winter- ................................................................. 61

**Swiss Architecture** ............................................... **63**

**Famous Switzerland Landmarks** ......................... **66**

1. Bellinzona Castles ..................................... 66

2. Chapel Bridge in Lucerne ......................... 67

3. Chillon Castle ............................................ 69

4. Gruyere Medieval Castle ........................... 70

5. Jet D'eau Geneva ....................................... 72

6. Lavaux Vineyard Terraces ........................ 73

7. Mount Pilatus ............................................ 74

8. Mount Titlis ............................................... 75

9. Rhine Falls ................................................. 77

10. Schilthorn-Piz Gloria ............................... 78

11. Schäfler Ridge ........................................... 80

12. Sphinx Observatory at Jungfraujoch ...... 82

13. St. Peterskirche in Zurich ........................ 83

14. The Abbey of St. Gall ............................... 85

15. The First Cliff Walk in Grindelwald ....... 87

16. The Lion Monument in Lucerne ............ 88

17. The Glacier Express Trainline ................ 89

18. The Matterhorn ........................................ 91

**Switzerland Flora & Fauna** .................................. **93**

## Switzerland's Best Zoos and Aquariums ............ 96
Zoo Zurich ................................................................. 96
Falconeria Locarno ..................................................... 97
Zoo Basel ..................................................................... 98
Aquatis Aquarium-Vivarium Lausanne ..................... 99
Tierpark Bern ............................................................ 100
Natur- und Tierpark Goldau .................................... 100

## Best Traditional Events in Switzerland ............. 103
1. Basel Carnival ...................................................... 103
2. Sechseläuten ........................................................ 105
3. Finale Nationale de la Race d'Hérens ................. 105
4. Swiss Yodeling Festival ....................................... 107
5. International Alphorn Festival ........................... 107
6. Swiss National Day ............................................. 108
7. Schwägalp Schwinget .......................................... 109
8. Cattle Descent .................................................... 109
9. Chestnut Festival ................................................ 111
10. Zibelemärit ........................................................ 111
11. Fête de l'Escalade .............................................. 113

## First-Time Visit to Switzerland - What to Expect + Travel Tips ...................................................... 115

## References ........................................................... 124

Switzerland is a country centralized in the continent of Europe. It is connected to five other countries by a 1,935 km long border: Italy, France, Germany, Austria, and the Principality of Liechtenstein. Switzerland is geographically divided into three distinct regions—approximately 58% of the land is inhabited by the Alps, the second largest region is the Central Plateau at about 31%, and the Jura at 11%. Switzerland is recognizable by its mountain peaks at least 4,000 meters tall, also known as the 49 four-thousanders. Although the Alps are the most extensive region in the country, it is only inhabited by a population of 11%.

# The Swiss Alps

The Alps are a primary tourist destination in Switzerland and the country most popularly associated with this beautiful mountainous region. Some of the most famous Alpine destinations are in Switzerland, such as the Matterhorn, the Eiger, the Jungfrau, and various tallest peaks and glaciers. A complex network of adequately marked hiking trails is also available to tourists visiting the Alps.

## Facts about the Mountains

» Most of the Alps' 4,000-meter peaks (48 of 82) are found throughout Switzerland, with the remaining few within 20 km of the Swiss border.
» The Monte Rosa is the tallest summit in the Swiss Alps, reaching 4,634 meters (15, 202 ft.), and is located on the Switzerland-Italy border.

- » The Dom is located solely in the Swiss region, the tallest mountain at 4,545 meters (14,911 ft.).
- » The Ascona, located in the canton of Ticino, is the lowest point in Switzerland, only reaching 643 ft. (196 meters) above sea level. The Ascona is only 43 miles (70 km) from the Monte Rosa summit.
- » The Haute Route begins at Chamonix and ends at Zermatt, passing through the Alps' twelve tallest peaks.

## Facts about the Glaciers

- » 3% of the Swiss territory, or an area of 1,230 km², is covered in glaciers and equates to 44% of the total glaciated land within the Alps (2800 km²).
- » The Aletsch Glacier is the Alps' largest glacier (translated to Aletschgletscher in German), is roughly 23 km in length, and has over 120 square kilometers of land coverage (over 45 square miles). The Aletsch is located in the canton of Valais within the Bernese Alps.
- » The Swiss Alps are home to the most numerous concentration of glaciers.

# Facts about the Hiking Trails

- » An extensive network of walking trails is located in Switzerland, measuring 62,000 km. The mountainous regions are the location of 23,000 km total of walking trails.
- » The tallest European summit served by cable car is the Klein Matterhorn, close to Zermatt. The cable car terminal is at an elevation of 3,820 meters (12,533 feet).
- » Switzerland's lifestyle is based on walking and hiking, with approximately 9,650 daily steps (roughly 5 miles) for the average Swiss person. On the other hand, 5,117 daily steps (or 2.5 miles) are what the average American walks.

Switzerland's territory is covered 7.5% of settlement areas, which are purposed for housing, infrastructure (such as trade, industry, and transportation), water and energy stock, wastewater removal, and eco-friendly and recreational destinations. Roughly 40% of Swiss territory is dedicated to agriculture, while forest and woodland make up approximately 30% of Swiss land. Most of Switzerland's natural forest re-growth takes place at prior mountain pastures.

Approximately 4% of Switzerland's land comprises about 1,500 lakes combined with other bodies of water, such as streams and lakes. Within the Gotthard massif, deep in the Swiss Alps, are the Rhine, Rhone, Reuss, and Ticino—four of Switzerland's primary rivers. Moreover, 6% of Europe's freshwater reserves are located in Switzerland. The sources of extensive European rivers such as the Rhone, Rhine, and Inn are in the Swiss Alps. The Ticino River is a tributary of the Po (Italy), while the Inn flows through the Danube (Germany).

# Facts about Switzerland's Primary Rivers

### The Rhine River

» **The Rhine River travels through six different countries.** Since Roman times, the Rhine River has served as a connector between north and south Europe. From the

Swiss Alps, it travels through Switzerland, Germany, Austria, the Netherlands, France, and the Principality of Liechtenstein.

» **The Rhine River is a popularly traveled European river.** Over 1,600 barges transporting 500 million tonnes of cargo daily traverse the river. The scenic views around the river, including cliffside castles, vineyards, and towns, make it a desirable choice for European cruise lines. At the height of the cruise season, over 300 river cruise ships sail along the Rhine River.

## The Rhone River

» **The Rhone River is a historical trade route.** Since the historical period of the ancient Greeks and Romans, the Rhone has served as a crucial trade route, linking the eastern and central regions of the Roman province of Gaul to the Mediterranean. In addition, ports and various cities are connected by the Rhone River, including Avignon, Vienne, and Arles.

» **The Rhone River flows through Switzerland and France.** As the second largest river in France at roughly 504 miles total, the Rhone River begins at the Rhone Glacier in the Swiss Alps (within the canton of Valais). Its initial flow is generally northwest through Lake Geneva, then meanders toward the southwest from Switzerland to France, joining with the Saône River in the Lyon vicinity.

## The Reuss River

- » **The Reuss is a popular bathing destination.** It has become a highly-desired bathing spot in recent years, thanks to the downstream current that allows people to float freely.
- » **It is also a popular canoeing tour hotspot.** Beginning in the historic and scenic town of Bremgarten, the Reuss River becomes an ideal location for canoeing tours, where the natural landscape is practically untouched. Gebenstorf is the tour's ending point, just before the Aare and Reuss connect.

## The Ticino River

- » **The banks of the Ticino are home to several beloved attractions.** Tourists are often attracted by the prominent sights here, such as the Romanesque church of San Nicolao in Giornico and Bellinzona's three castles considered UNESCO World Heritage Sites. The Ticino River then flows along the Magadino Plain and Lago Maggiore.

- » **The Ticino River has breathtaking waterfalls.** Beginning at Biasca, tourists can marvel at Ticino's highest waterfalls. The Santa Petronilla Waterfalls divides into three stages as it passes through the valley. The second waterfall, Bolle di Magadino, where its pristine wetlands are the resting point for over 200 species of migrating birds before they venture through the Swiss Alps.

## Switzerland Geography – Other Key Facts and Information

- » From north to south, Switzerland is 220 km in measurement, and from east to west, it is 348 km in size.
- » The Dufourspitze, within the Monte Rosa massif, is Switzerland's tallest peak and measures 4,634m above sea level.
- » The Graubünden canton features over 1,200 mountain peaks reaching at least 2,000m high.
- » Forty-eight mountain peaks at a minimum of 4,000 meters high are found in Switzerland.
- » Switzerland's lowest point, Lake Maggiore, reaches only 193m above sea level.
- » Europe's highest railway station, the Jungfraujoch, is 3,454m above sea level in the Bern canton.

- » The highest village in Switzerland, Juf, is 2,126m above sea level within the canton of Graubünden.
- » Switzerland is home to roughly 20% of the Alps in total.
- » Europe's most expansive glacier, the Aletsch Glacier, expands over 23 km within the Valais canton.
- » Switzerland's landscape is covered by approximately 1,000 km² of glaciers. However, between 1985–2009, they melted by as much as 390 km².
- » Located 2,883m above sea level, the Monte Rosa Hut is bordered by glaciers and the formidable Valais Alps peaks.
- » 12 UNESCO World Heritage Sites are located in Switzerland, such as the Jungfrau–Aletsch region, the Albula and Bernina lines of the Rhaetian Railways, and Monte San Giorgio.

# THE SWISS PLATEAU

The densest populated region in Switzerland is the Central Plateau, also known as the "Mittelland" (middle country). Beginning at Lake Geneva from the southwest and ending at Lake Constance from the northeast.

Almost 50 percent of this region's land is dedicated to intensive farming, while forests cover another 24 percent. Sixteen percent of the land use in the Central Plateau is dedicated to settlement areas, which is more than the national average by double. Regarding Switzerland's total land coverage, settlement areas account for approximately 7.7 percent or 3,000 km².

The Jura and the Rhine flank the northern end of the Central Plateau, while Lake Geneva and the Swiss Alps flank the southern end. Despite the Central Plateau encompassing roughly 30% of Switzerland's land, it is densely populated, with over two-thirds of its total population.

# Switzerland's Most-Produced Agriculture Commodities

1. **Raw cattle milk:** The most significant agricultural commodity in Switzerland is cattle milk as of 2020. Milk production from cattle yielded 3,765,000 tonnes, as confirmed by the FAO Statistical Corporate Database (FAOSTAT). Certain cattle species in Swiss are known to produce larger quantities of milk, such as the Swiss Holstein, Simmental, Swiss Fleckvieh, and Jersey cow. Switzerland is also home to well-known dairy companies such as Emmi AG, Von Muhlenen, and Nestle.
2. **Sugar beet:** As of 2020, sugar beet is Switzerland's second largest agricultural commodity. According to the FAOSTAT, 1,423,529 tonnes was the production yield of sugar beet. Northern Switzerland is the primary cultivation region of sugar beet.
3. **Wheat:** In Switzerland, wheat is the third most widely produced agricultural commodity as of 2020. Wheat production reached 527,496 tonnes, according to FAOSTAT. Switzerland has a few primary cultivation regions for wheat, including Bern, Fribourg, Vaud, and Aargau.

4. **Potatoes:** As of 2020, potatoes are another significant agricultural commodity in Switzerland, and their production reached 490,000 tonnes, according to the FAOSTAT. Cultivation of potatoes in Switzerland requires roughly 10,000 hectares of land.
5. **Bone-in pig meat, fresh or chilled:** Pig meat is Switzerland's fifth most-produced agricultural commodity as of 2020, with production reaching 223,986 tonnes, according to the FAOSTAT. Switzerland's most favorable pig species for meat production include the Swiss Edelschwein, Duroc, and Swiss Landrasse.
6. **Maize (corn):** As of 2020, corn is Switzerland's sixth most-produced agricultural commodity, with a production level of 219,692 tonnes. Switzerland's primary regions for corn production are Ticino, Valle Mesolcina, and specific areas of Valais.
7. **Apples:** The seventh most-produced agricultural commodity in Switzerland is apples, as of 2020. Apple production reached 192,443 tonnes, according to the FAOSTAT. Specific regions within Switzerland are home to apple orchards, including Thurgau, Zug, Zurich, Aargau, Valais, Vaud, and St. Gallen.

8. **Barley:** As of 2020, Switzerland's 8th most-produced agricultural commodity is barley, reaching a production level of 192,024 tonnes. A few cultivation regions of barley include Vaud, Bern, Zurich, Fribourg, and Aargau.
9. **Bone-in cattle meat, fresh or chilled:** Cattle meat is Switzerland's 9th most-produced agricultural commodity as of 2020. One hundred forty-three thousand six hundred sixty-three tonnes is the total production statistic of cattle meat. Specific cattle species are better suited for meat production, which includes Herens, Swiss Fleckvieh, Simmental, and Evolene.
10. **Grapes:** As of 2020, grapes are Switzerland's 10th most-produced agricultural commodity. The statistical production of grapes reached 105,739 tonnes, according to FAOSTAT. In addition, certain indigenous species of grapes are planted in Switzerland, and these cultivars include Cornalin, Petite Arvine, and Humagne Rouge. Wine production in Switzerland occurs in Lake Geneva's southern regions, in the Valais.

# The Swiss Jura

Western Switzerland is occupied by the Jura Mountains, with its extensive sweeping arc reaching out from the Rhone River close to Geneva over to the Rhine. It has a range of over 200 miles that straddles most of the France-Swiss border. The Jura landscape is occasionally referred to as the *arc jurassien,* a notable geographic attraction in Switzerland. The Jura is occupied alongside the Alps and Swiss Plateau, forming a natural barrier between Switzerland and France.

The Jura is worthy of recognition thanks to its great cycling and hiking trails and its peaceful, one-of-a-kind Swiss experience with an abundance of mellow hills, medieval-style towns, windy peaks, flourishing orchards, and tranquil valleys surrounded by quiet farming villages that embrace down to earth lifestyle. In addition, the Jura is a fantastic destination for French-inspired cuisine.

The primary language in the Jura region is French, which correlates directly with the lively cafe culture.

However, toward the northeast mountains, the primary language spoken becomes German. This unseen divider between the languages is humorously known as *Röstigraben* by the locals.

A unique characteristic of the area near *Röstigraben* is that the places' names are written in German and French. For example, the nearby town of Biel is also called Bienne. Murten, another town referred to as such by German speakers, is also called Morat by the French. The Jura region is widely referred to as *la frontière* by the locals, a suitable name for an area that encompasses a variety of language and cultural differences, occasionally amongst the same city council chambers.

A satisfying aspect of the Jura is its wide variety of characteristics while traversing from the northeast down to the southwest. Nature reserves and protected areas dot the Jura, eco-consciously secured to maintain the protection of local wildlife and flowering plant life. Additionally, the Jura is famously known for growing up to 950 species of flowering plants, including vast forests, thanks to its limestone base.

Vastly available throughout the UK, delicatessens is also a delicacy in the Jura region known as Vacherin Mont d'Or, an oven-baked soft cheese served on top of boiled potatoes. This cheese is recognizable by its distinguished flavor, encased in locally felled spruce. A love for geology is at the heart of the Jura, thanks to its vast array of scenic wonders ranging from the Creux du Van, Dent de

Vaulion, Aiguille de Baulmes, and La Dôle as being the most notable destinations. Sitting above the town of Noiraigue within a valley, the Creux du Van is a prime example of Jura limestone that features a half-mile long, 160m tall vertical rocky wall amphitheater. Furthermore, gorgeous scenery is also provided by the Jura Trail traveling along the top of the natural auditorium.

## The Jura Crest Trail

The Jura Crest Trail is one of Switzerland's seven designated long-distance hiking trails. Commonly known as the classic Swiss long-distance path, several waymakers have plotted the route since 1905, resulting in hassle-free and straightforward navigation.

Expanding for 192 miles of the Jura Mountains, the Jura Crest Trail begins nine miles away from Zurich at the quaint town of Dielsdorf to Nyon, nestled on Lake Geneva's shores. Venturing on this trail takes roughly two weeks on average and is best suited for experienced travelers of at least moderate fitness, as the daily journey is a challenge with up to 20 miles of trail length and a height gain of up to 1,700m in a single day. Easy to moderate hiking paths feature over 13,800m of ascent through the 192-mile venture.

Despite reaching challenging distances and heights, taking in the wondrous scenery of the Jura Mountains is a worthy reward, along with the Alps' peaks and ridges and the Rhone Valley. Along with a fun and relaxing adventure, the trail is accessible to most and features local shops/amenities just off the path.

Ease of travel is also guaranteed for hikers seeking to explore the Jura Crest Trail, thanks to the trail being broken up into 14 stages which vary depending on individual fitness needs. In addition, thanks to its proximity to civilization, accommodations either on or close to the trail are available for travelers, such as Swiss Alpine Club huts which are self-catering and affordable compared to hotels. Camping and hostel accommodations are also available, featuring a wide variety of bed and breakfast options.

# Switzerland Culture

Diversity is the hallmark feature of Switzerland's culture, as the country is centralized amongst various outstanding European cultures. Being a multilingual nation, the primary languages spoken in Switzerland are German, Italian, French, and Romansh, with several dialects spoken in specific regions and unique cultural features found in each canton. Furthermore, individual regions in Switzerland are home to their unique cultures, customs, and traditions.

A notable cultural distinction in Switzerland is between the mountain valley lifestyle in the mountains and the city lifestyle of the central plateau. Additionally, as time and tourism increased, certain local customs became the subject of national fame. The Swiss Alps are crucial to Switzerland's history and cultural diversity.

It's crucial to consider that Swiss culture adheres to the old-aged traditions regardless of the influence of tourism. Prideful and traditional, the Swiss people are lovers and folk music performers, resembling lively dance music. Switzerland's vibrant music scene has dominated throughout the cantons. Over time, Alpine folk music has flourished in the verbal form of skills and compositions, passing between generations as the decades and even centuries passed.

Swiss culture's most widely used musical instruments include the accordion (Schwyzeroergeli), clarinet dulcimer (Jew's harp), violin, and bass violin. In addition, another instrument of significant cultural importance is the alphorn, which was previously used as a signaling instrument among herders. Per the rules of Switzerland, a choir or traditional music band belongs to every village in the country.

Arts and crafts, particularly watchmaking, is a famous cultural aspect of Switzerland, and the industry of Swiss watches has flourished with an honorable reputation over the passing decades. An impressive collection of 4500 timepieces and over 700 wall clocks is featured at La-Chaux-de-Fonds International Clock Museum. Additionally, visitors to the clock museum may enjoy the relaxing ambiance of these clocks ticking.

Switzerland is a phenomenal destination for lovers of various arts, and visitors can observe the country's cultural origins in over 600 museums. Some of the most famous museums are described as follows:

# Swiss National Museum

**Address:** Museumstrasse 2, 8001 Zürich, Switzerland

**Price:** $10 Swiss francs (roughly $11) for adults, free admission for Zurich card holders and children 16 or younger

**Hours:** Tuesday–Sunday 10 a.m.–5 p.m., Thursday 10 a.m.–7 p.m.

**Suggested Duration:** Between 2 hours and half a day

**Official Website:** https://www.landesmuseum.ch/en

Located in the northern tip of Kreis 1, the Switzerland National Museum resides in a historical building with a castle architectural style featuring surveys of Swiss art, culture, and history dating way back to the 4th century B.C. Exhibits of varying interests are featured here, such as religious and medieval frescoes, unique weapons, and Swiss-designed furniture. Additionally, visitors can explore several various ornate rooms during their stay.

According to prior visitors, one of the most notable features of the Switzerland National Museum is the captivating architectural design, along with an extensive, well-detailed layout of Switzerland's history. However, to fully enjoy the unique experiences at this museum, it's recommended to utilize a free English audio guide online since German is the language written on most of the museum's displays.

In addition to observing many exciting displays, museum tickets grant access to bathrooms, a gift shop, a library, and a cafe. Although onsite parking isn't available at the Switzerland National Museum, parking access is located at the Hauptbahnhof train station across the street. Hauptbahnhof or the adjacent Bahnhofquai station can also access various trains, trams, and bus lines.

## Kunstmuseum Basel

**Address:** St. Alban-Graben 16, 4051 Basel, Switzerland

**Price:** Adults 20 and over, 26 Swiss francs for an all-in-one special exhibition including collection & exhibitions, 16 Swiss francs without special exhibition

**Hours:** 10 a.m.–8 p.m. daily

**Suggested Duration:** 2–3 hours

**Official Website:** https://kunstmuseumbasel.ch/

One of the most extensive and long-preserved art collections in Europe is found at Kunstmuseum Basel, with a unique history featuring works dating from the early fifteenth century to the modern day.

The museum is split into two separate areas: the Galerie (Gallery) and the Kupferstichkabinett (Department of Prints and Drawings). Paintings and drawings created by active artists between 1400 and 1600 in the Upper Rhine region and of the 19th and 21st centuries are the primary focus of Kunstmuseum Basel's displays.

Visitors can find the most extensive collection of works created by the Holbein family here. Other significant Renaissance art examples are featured by masters, including Konrad Witz, Lucas Cranach the Elder, Martin Schongauer, and Matthias Grünewald. Basilius Amerbach, a lawyer based in Basel, was the original collector of most of these works of art. Upon their purchase in 1661 by the city, these works of art established the framework of the world's first municipal museum open to the public.

Featured amongst 19th-century highlights are paintings created by Basel-native Arnold Böcklin. The primary accent of 20th-century art focuses on Cubism (Picasso, Braque, Léger), Abstract Expressionism, German Expressionism, and American art beginning in 1950.

## Lucerne Transportation Museum

**Address:** Lidostrasse 5, 6006 Luzern, Switzerland

**Price:** Adults 32 Swiss francs, kids 14 Swiss francs, free admission for children under 6

**Hours:** Daily 10 a.m.–6 p.m. (until 5 p.m. during winter)

**Suggested Duration:** 5 hours

**Official Website:**
https://www.verkehrshaus.ch/en/home.html

Travelers interested in anything related to planes, trains, cars, boats, space travel, and other modes of transportation will enjoy the experiences offered at the Lucerne Transportation Museum, also known as *Verkehrshaus*. Not only is it Switzerland's most famous museum, but a variety of indoor halls are available to explore in this vast complex, with a different type of travel as the focal point in each. Kids can also enjoy an educational experience thanks to many hands-on interactive displays with informative material.

The Lucerne Transportation Museum takes a hands-on approach by offering a supervised driving course outside, plenty of complimentary scooters for guests to traverse the museum grounds, a construction-zone play space for children, etc. Additional features include a Planetarium and IMAX theater. However, outdoor activities may be temporarily closed during off-seasons and extreme weather conditions.

# The Olympic Museum

**Address:** Quai d'Ouchy 1, 1006 Lausanne, Switzerland

**Price:** Adults (aged 16+) 18 Swiss francs, child (up to 15) accompanied by an adult, free admission

**Hours:** Tuesday–Sunday, 9 a.m.–6 p.m. Closed on Mondays

**Suggested Duration:** 2 hours

**Official Website:** https://olympics.com/museum

An up-close experience to see the Olympics and be in touch with the sporting spirit much like athletes are, a trip to Lausanne's Olympic Museum is well worth the visit. The experience at The Olympic Museum is complete with 3000 m² of exhibition space, 1,500+ exhibits, and 150 viewing screens. Additionally, advanced computer technology and audiovisual media allow visitors to understand the Olympics' history from its origins to the modern day.

Pierre de Coubertin is responsible for the founding idea of a museum showcasing and paying respect to the Olympic games. Furthermore, he is also the founder of the International Olympic Committee (IOC), and he restored the Olympic Games. Established in 1993 in the Lausanne district of Ouchy, The Olympic Museum is a reflection of the sports spirit which brings the competitive passion of nations together.

Located in the most pristine location of Lake Geneva, an extraordinary new building features interactive exhibitions, films, documents, and an assortment of exquisite items originating from Greek antiquity to the modern day. Individuals seeking information on all subject matter of the Olympic Games will learn plenty of knowledge at the museum, which houses the most extensive collection of information worldwide.

Visitors can indulge in a delicious brunch at the TOM Café on Saturdays and Sundays while enjoying the stunning scenery of Lake Geneva and the surrounding mountains. In addition, the cuisine of cities that have hosted the Olympic Games is the inspiration for the menus at TOM Café.

# Red Cross and Red Crescent International Museum

**Address:** Av. de la Paix 17, 1202 Genève, Switzerland

**Price:** Adults 15 Swiss francs, free admission for children and visitors with a Geneva City Pass discount

**Hours:** April–October: 10 a.m.–6 p.m.

November–March: 10 a.m.–5 p.m.

Closed on Mondays

**Suggested Duration:** 1 hour

**Official Website:** https://www.ifrc.org/

The Red Cross and Red Crescent International Museum will take its visitors through the history of humanitarianism and invoke emotion, discovery, and reflection in the process. One hundred fifty years of humanitarian history unfolded through an interactive chronology. In addition, visitors can view real-time operations conducted by Red Cross and Red Crescent worldwide.

Designed by a famous exhibition architect, three individual sections of the museum allow its guests to analyze three significant challenges of the modern world: protecting human dignity, reviving family links, and limiting natural risks. Combined with traditional museography, an adventurous experience is part of the museum's exhibition, inspiring visitors to fulfill contemporary humanitarian action.

The initial phase of each zone is directed at increasing an individual's awareness which commonly brings forth a powerful emotional experience. The second stage provides visitors with the historical origins and information about the Red Cross, reminding them that it is the earliest and most substantial international humanitarian organization. And lastly, the next zone features an "On The Spot" area, a grand interactive globe that allows visitors to see real-time activity and news from the field.

# Swiss Cuisine

At the heart of Swiss culture is its delicious cuisine, which is undoubtedly heaven on Earth for foodies. In addition to its original dishes, Switzerland is a mixing pot of the best culinary traditions from neighboring countries, including German, French, and North Italian cuisine. This culinary diversity is why Swiss cuisine varies significantly by region; therefore, specific national dishes or traditional Swiss food hardly exist.

With historical origins as a farming country, Switzerland's dishes are ordinary and prepared with simple ingredients. Although meal ingredients and preparation methods vary throughout the country, tourists can spot certain peculiarities. For example, several of Switzerland's most popular dishes are combinations of potatoes, meats, and cheeses served with various sauces, with their preparation regarded as a high standard of art.

The influence of specific dishes has made them famous nationwide favorites throughout Switzerland, despite culinary specialties that differentiate by region. One of these is a highly regarded dish made with cheese fondue. It is melted cheese served with dried cubes of bread in a traditional pot called "caquelon." The key to making this dish memorable is figuring out the ideal balance of flavors and cheese. In addition, fondue is best enjoyed on cold winter days in a comfortable atmosphere.

Raclette is another favorite cheese in Switzerland. A cow's milk cheese is heated and cooked on a stove before the melted part is scraped off the bottom of the pan. It is then typically served with gherkins, potatoes, and onions. Another adored dish is Roesti, prepared from grated, cooked potatoes, then fried in butter or oil. Initially, the families of farmers in the Bern canton served and ate

Roesti as a breakfast dish. Despite being regarded as a food consumed by the impoverished residing in the German region of Switzerland, it started the concept of the Roesti Curtain (Roesti Graben), which has evolved into the cultural meeting point between the population of the German-speaking and French-speaking.

Also worth mentioning is a classic invented in Switzerland around the 1900s called muesli. This breakfast dish is centered around rolled oats, served with either cow's milk or soymilk, fresh or dried fruits, yogurt, or nuts and seeds.

The Swiss people are known for and pride themselves on their high-quality chocolates and cheeses, with Emmentaler cheese, Swiss Gruyere, Cailler chocolate, and Lindt chocolate being famous worldwide. However, when it comes to local specialties in Switzerland, Basel is home to Laeckerli, Aargau is home to Rueeblitorte, and Zug is home to the cherry cake.

# Other Traditional Swiss Foods Worth Trying

1. **Tarts and Quiches:** These two dishes are only technically superficially related since they are both prepared with cheese, custard, and pastry. However, what sets them apart is the custard is the primary focus of the quiche,

whereas cheese is the greater focus of the Swiss tart.

Despite being available in various sizes, the more eye-pleasing and petite tarts are on the smaller side, which is bite-sized and can be eaten picnic-style. In addition, miniature cheese tarts have a festive appeal and are a great accessory to small, decorative plates. While tarts can be sweet or savory and topped with different flavors, including onion to sweet apple, you may prepare quiches with fish, meat, or vegetables. Tarts and quiches are commonly served for birthdays and anniversaries.

2. **Landjager:** As a popular carry-on snack for hikers in Switzerland, landjager is a semi-dried sausage prepared with a blend of pork, beef, lard, sugar, select spices, and red wine. The name of this traditional Swiss snack translates to land hunters, which is a reference to the fact that they are a popular convenience amongst backpackers and hunters who travel with them on the go.

3. **Älpermagronen (Alpine Macaroni):** Translated to 'the Alpine macaroni,' Älpermagronen is a rustic dish from Switzerland. Its name is historical since its ingredients are what herders ate while keeping watch of their cows as they grazed in

the Alp's pastures. Since its origins in the 1930s, Älplermagronen has been known as one of Switzerland's most flavorful traditional cuisines. Its primary ingredients are macaroni pasta, onions, potatoes, and cheese, although numerous variations of this classic Swiss dish exist.

4. **Saffron Risotto:** Swiss saffron is famously regarded as among the most premium, expensive saffron worldwide. Saffron risotto is in high demand due to dark red saffron strands being the stigma of various crocus and being hand-picked. Saffron is cultivated in the Valais canton, while saffron risotto is primarily regarded as a traditional dish in Ticino and is typically served with a raw sausage prepared from pork, red wine, and spices known as Luganighe. Saffron risotto is also highly customizable, with onions being a popular ingredient in the cooking process.

5. **Zürcher Geschnetzeltes:** Also known as Zurich Ragout, this white-sauce-based stew dish is prepared with mushrooms and white wine. Several popular German flavorings, such as lemon zest and parsley, are involved in the preparation. Although it may look gourmet, the cooking process is quite simple and traditionally calls for veal loin; however, pork loin may be a substitute. Swiss hash

browns, also known as Rösti, and a Swiss white wine are the typical sides served with Zurich Ragout. It was first mentioned in a 1947 cookbook, with the original ingredients being sliced strips of veal, cream, white wine, and demiglace. However, mushrooms and sliced veal kidneys are also mentioned in specific contemporary recipes.

# Switzerland's Best Restaurants - Top 10

### Vieux Chalet (Best for Raclette)

**Address:** Untere Dorfstrasse 30, 3906 Saas-Fee, Switzerland

**Price Range:** $16–$49

**Cuisine Type:** European, Swiss, Vegetarian-Friendly

**Hours:** 5 p.m.–11:30 p.m.

**Official Website:** https://www.vieux-chalet-saas-fee.ch/

Saas-Fee's cozy and charming village of Alpine is home to the lovely Vieux Chalet restaurant, located in the town's historic center, which is famous for its delicious raclette. This melted cheese is served with potatoes, bread, gherkins, and pearl onions on a plate. The best part of this dining experience is watching the raclette being carved off a massive wheel of melting cheese.

## Le Chalet de Gruyères (Best for Fondue)

**Address:** Rle des Chevaliers 1, 1663 Gruyères, Switzerland

**Price Range:** $27–$49

**Cuisine Type:** Swiss-European, Vegetarian-Friendly

**Hours:** 9 a.m.–9 p.m. Sunday–Thursday, 9 a.m.–9 p.m. Friday–Saturday

**Official Website:**
https://www.gruyereshotels.ch/chalet-de-gruyeres/

Customers can enjoy Switzerland's most top-rated fondue at Chalet de Gruyères. Located in the cheese-making heart of Gruyères, this restaurant provides all the authentic cheesiness that is sure to impress its guests' taste buds. Paired with local wine and beer, local dried meats, fondue, and raclette are all worth a try. Decadently delicious desserts also feature double Gruyères cream.

## Zeughauskeller (Best for Hearty Swiss Fare)

**Address:** Bahnhofstrasse 28A, 8001 Zürich, Switzerland

**Price Range:** $$–$$$

**Cuisine Type:** German, Swiss, European

**Hours:** 11:30 a.m.–11 p.m.

**Official Website:**
https://www.zeughauskeller.ch/home

One of the best restaurants in Zurich, Zeughauskeller is a fusion of a great atmosphere, history, and delicious meat-centric specialties within German-speaking Switzerland. Main courses include Wienerschnitzel, pork shanks, steaks, and meter-long sausages, with potato salad, rösti potatoes, French fries, or side salads as side dishes. Combined with rich, hearty fare, guests can enjoy the ambiance of this massive dining hall, which was initially a weapons armory from the 15th century. To avoid a long line of customers, arriving slightly early or later for lunch and dinner is best.

## Tea Room Frutal (Best for Desserts)

**Address:** Bahnhofstrasse 18, 3860 Meiringen, Switzerland

**Price Range:** $$–$$$

**Cuisine Type:** Swiss, Cafe, Vegetarian-Friendly

**Hours:** 7 a.m.–12 p.m., 1:30 p.m.–6:15 p.m. Monday–Friday, 7 a.m.–5:15 p.m. Saturday, 8 a.m.–5:15 p.m. Sunday

**Official Website:** https://frutal.ch/

It's been said that Meiringen, Switzerland is the birthplace of the sweet, baked egg white dessert known as meringue, so the nation's most famous meringue confectioner is unsurprisingly operated here. The eatery is also hard to miss, with its massive meringue beckoning customers out front. A fusion between a bakery, tea room, and dessert house, tasty sweets such as chocolate confections, creamy pastries, and apple strudels are served here. In addition, holiday-themed treats are a kid favorite here.

## Brasserie Lipp (Best for Classic French Cuisine)

**Address:** Confédération centre, Rue de la Confédération 8, 1204 Geneva, Switzerland

**Price:** $$–$$$

**Cuisine Type:** French, Seafood, European

**Hours:** 8 a.m.–12 a.m. Sunday–Wednesday, 8 a.m.–1 a.m. Thursday–Saturday

**Official Website:** https://www.brasserie-lipp.com/

Since French is the first language spoken in Geneva, there are many premium-quality French restaurants in the region. Still, very few offer the classic authenticity found at Brasserie Lipp, which, appearance-wise, looks like it came from Paris' Left Bank. This lively, multi-room eatery serves oysters, moules frites, escargot, and beef tartare. Despite seafood being this restaurant's primary cuisine, many turf-based dishes are also served to customers.

## Findlerhof (Best Dining with a View)

**Address:** Findeln 2051m, Zermatt 3920 Switzerland

**Price:** $$$$

**Cuisine Type:** Swiss, European, Central European

**Hours:** 11:30 a.m.–4 p.m.

**Official Website:** https://www.findlerhof.ch/

Located in the car-free, miniature food hamlet of Findeln, this rustic restaurant is available via cable car, funicular, or an incredibly steep hike uphill. As a result, it is more frequently visited by guests on their way down the mountain rather than on the way up. Sunny terraces and a woodsy design are the ideal atmospheres for traditional pasta, risottos, rösti, and meaty dishes. The food may attract customers at Findlerhof, but its spectacular views will keep them staying. When the clouds part and the sky is clear, the magnificent Matterhorn mightily looms across the valley, providing the most classical Swiss panoramas in the region.

## Haus Hiltl, Zurich (Best Vegetarian Dining)

**Address:** Sihlstrasse 28, Zurich 8001 Switzerland

**Price:** $$–$$$

**Cuisine Type:** Indian, Swiss, Mediterranean

**Hours:** 7 a.m.–10 p.m. Monday–Thursday, 7 a.m.–11 p.m. Friday, 8 a.m.–11 p.m. Saturday, 10 a.m.–10 p.m. Sunday

**Official Website:** https://hiltl.ch/

Founded as the longest-running and likely the first vegetarian restaurant before vegetarianism became popular, Hiltl was established in 1898 with delicious menu options that cater to both vegetarians and vegans alike, and even lifelong meat eaters may be persuaded by their hearty potato truffle soup or the smoked tofu prepared with red wine sauce known as the Hiltl Wellington. Hiltl has several establishments throughout Zurich, while the flagship restaurant is located a few blocks from Zurich HB train station at the Sihlstrasse 28 address.

## The Restaurant at the Chedi (Best International Dining)

**Address:** Gotthardstrasse 4, 6490 Andermatt, Switzerland

**Price:** $22–$540

**Cuisine Type:** Swiss, Sushi, European, Asian

**Hours:** 7 a.m.–11 a.m., 12 p.m.–2 p.m., 6:30 p.m.–10 p.m.

**Official Website:**
https://www.thechediandermatt.com/dining/the-restaurant

A unique find in the middle of a Swiss ski resort is the Restaurant at the Chedi Andermatt, which creatively fuses Indian, Vietnamese, Thai, and European cuisines into an original menu full of variety. Chedi's relaxed, down-to-earth atmosphere is ideal for indulging in specialties such as Thai beef salad or murgh makhani. The dining experience here is topped off with the Swiss-based wine and cheese tower standing 16 feet tall.

# Switzerland's Climate

Switzerland experiences moderate, agreeable winters and summers due to the country's location in a temperate climate zone. However, weather and climate change vary significantly depending on the altitude. The Atlantic Ocean dramatically influences the climate in Switzerland's western and north-western regions. Westerly winds deliver a moderate, humid sea breeze to the country. However, the Mediterranean Sea holds significant influence over Switzerland's southern region.

The Alps are essential to climate development since they separate the country into various climatic zones and act as a natural barrier between Switzerland's northern and southern regions. Seventy-eight inches of precipitation annually is the average amount for the northern area of Switzerland. At the same time, the southern part receives approximately 19 to 23 inches of rainfall annually, with the most rain occurring in the summer months.

During the winter, rain freezes into snowfall at an altitude of 1,200–1,500 meters above sea level. However, Switzerland's lowlands, such as certain low-lying western areas, the Basel area, and the greater Geneva area, are known to experience snowless winters.

Foehn wind is another climatic feature of Switzerland, which typically arrives during autumn and spring and crosses the Alps to bring mild and dry weather conditions. Along with recently apparent changes in Switzerland's seasons, there is significant variation between them. Even though Switzerland's winters were previously cold and snowy, this doesn't apply to the lowland regions. Several ski resorts nowadays rely on artificial snow to survive.

Greenery in nature thrives, and trees blossom in the springtime, but snowfall in April is no exception. Summer temperatures generally peak at 30 degrees Celsius (86 degrees Fahrenheit), but Switzerland has been known to get hotter during more extreme weather conditions. In autumn, various colors make for a lively landscape, and fruit is at the peak of ripeness.

Temperature range can vary greatly depending on the altitude, especially in the mountains. Therefore, hikers, campers, and mountain travelers are encouraged to pack durable walking shoes or boots, a sweater, sunglasses with built-in UV protection, sunscreen, and a light raincoat or compact umbrella.

Big cities such as Zurich, Geneva, Bern, and Lucerne are bustling during the two weeks of mid-December when Christmas is coming. December is ideal for travelers wishing to enjoy the Christmas and New Year holidays with family and friends. For those who love sports, outdoor activities in winter, and relaxing strolls through snow-covered cities, winter's peak season between January and February is the ideal time. These months are the coldest and with much shorter days.

Much like winter, Switzerland also gets its fair share of tourism in summer, with the warmest high season typically lasting from July to August. Although the weather may be too harsh for certain outdoor activities such as city tours, summer tourists can try sports such as biking, paragliding, and enjoying the views from Switzerland's most beautiful peaks. However, as long as you're prepared with appropriate travel items and dress for the season, a trip to Switzerland is fun any time of the year.

# Best Luxurious Hotels in Switzerland

## 1. Badrutt's Palace Hotel

**Key Specs:**

- » Free Wi-Fi: Yes
- » Resort Fee: No
- » Room Rate: $$$$

**Notable Amenities:** Breakfast with champagne daily, indoor infinity pool, Rolls-Royce transfers

**Address:** Via Serlas 27, 7500 St. Moritz, Switzerland

**Official Website:** https://badruttspalace.com/

When you envision the perfect vacation in the Swiss Alps, you probably dance with images of snow-capped villages and fireplace-filled hideaways. At Badrutt's Palace Hotel, you can experience this dream come true during an unbelievably luxurious stay in St. Moritz.

Reeling in travelers since 1896, this lakeside hotel continues to dazzle with mountain vistas, 13 restaurants and bars on-site, and a wide variety of activities ranging from winter skiing to summer paragliding.

Though the outdoor activities at Badrutt's Palace are more than adequate to preoccupy its guests, cozy indoor relaxation is also possible thanks to its 155 rooms and suites. Each room features a dramatic visual of either the village center (with a balcony upgrade) or Lake St. Moritz, as well as upholstered headboards, chandeliers designed from crystal, and freshly-flowered vases providing a fragrant flow of elegance. In addition, you'll wake up the next day rejuvenated and prepared to ride the slopes after a refreshing scalp massage from Palace Wellness spa.

## 2. The Dolder Grand

### Key Specs:

- » Free Wi-Fi: Yes
- » Resort Fee: No
- » Room Rate: $$$$

**Notable Amenities:** Free bike and BMW rentals, full-service spa, indoor and outdoor pools

**Address:** Kurhausstrasse 65, 8032 Zürich, Switzerland

**Official Website:** https://www.thedoldergrand.com/en/

The Dolder Grand is nestled on a hill overlooking Lake Zurich and is a palace-light establishment on the skyline of the financial center in Switzerland. Although the hotel maintains its distance from the busy lifestyle in Zurich, guests can conveniently access the Bahnhofstrasse via a private funicular—the ideal balance of solitude and convenience. Traditional turrets and timbered details are featured on the original building of 1899, but during its extensive renovation in 2008, two steel-and-glass wings were added, full of ultra-modern rooms.

Many stand-out features at the Dolder Grand can be enjoyed, such as a spa and golf course reaching 43,000 square feet. However, the massive art collection is the grandest of them all. A painting behind the front desk of Andy Warhol greets hotel guests, and they can marvel at over 100 additional works from Salvador Dalí and Takashi Murakami as they make their way through the grounds. The 175 rooms in the hotel vary in style and size—traditional, cozy rooms are offered at the original main building, while sleek decor and floor-to-ceiling windows are additions to the hotel wings.

## 3. The Woodward

### Key Specs:

- » Free Wi-Fi: Yes
- » Resort Fee: No
- » Room Rate: $$$$

**Notable Amenities:** Personal limousine transfers, cigar lounge, full-service Guerlain Spa

**Address:** Quai Wilson 37, 1201 Genève, Switzerland

**Official Website:** https://www.oetkercollection.com/hotels/the-woodward/

During its grand opening in 2021, Woodward was one of the finest hotels constructed. As an addition to the Oetker Collection, the property is nestled in a historic building originating in 1901 with a panoramic view of Lake Geneva, giving guests the feeling of lodging at a Belle Époque lake house, one adorned with wooden ebony walls, gilded mirrors, and chandeliers made out of Baccarat crystal. The opulence stretches out to all 26 suite-style rooms with fireplaces, silk wallpaper, and lake-view balconies.

Hotel guests can indulge in one of two fine-dining experiences elsewhere on the property: L'Atelier de Joël Robuchon and Le Jardinier, two outposts of the New York-based Michelin-star restaurants. An expansive wellness center is also featured at the hotel, fully equipped with a gym, multiple steam rooms, Swedish baths, a Guerlain spa, and the city's longest private indoor swimming pool. For guests feeling adventurous, you can inquire with the staff to set up a private boat tour on the lake or arrange a picnic at Le Jardinier to enjoy wine country.

# 4. Beau-Rivage Palace

## Key Specs:

- » Free Wi-Fi: Yes
- » Resort Fees: No
- » Room Rate: $$$

**Notable Amenities:** Dog-friendly rooms, Hamman spa, limousine airport transfers

**Address:** Chem. de Beau-Rivage 21, 1006 Lausanne, Switzerland

**Official Website:** https://www.brp.ch/en/home/

Located on Lake Geneva's shores, Beau-Rivage Palace's architectural design resembles something out of a fairy tale: acres of lush, serene garden, a beautiful Belle Époque facade, and outdoor pools glistening down the hillside. As a favorite haunt of Coco Chanel and Charlie Chaplin long ago, the hotel currently lures in crowds thanks to its two-Michelin-starred restaurant, spacious spa, and 168 immaculate rooms and suites.

Guests can choose a variety of rooms based on their preference: Lake Geneva, the Alps, or the city center of Lausanne, with specific spaces providing balconies and terraces. The style of accommodations varies, but lush textiles and patterned wallpaper should be expected, along with spacious soaking tubs with Cinq Mondes bath accessories. The hotel also offers its guests a wide array of fun activities, such as wintertime Christmas markets and summertime lake cruises.

# 5. The Chedi Andermatt

## Key Specs:

- » Free Wi-Fi: Yes
- » Resort Fees: No
- » Room Rate: $$$$

**Notable Amenities:** Ski butlers along with equipment rentals, complimentary breakfast, indoor and outdoor pools

**Address:** Gotthardstrasse 4, 6490 Andermatt, Switzerland

**Official Website:**
https://www.thechediandermatt.com/

Andermatt, nestled in the heart of the Swiss Alps as a laid-back ski village, is the perfect contrast that flaunts the striking Asian-inspired Chedi Andermatt in a flashy fashion. Owned by GHM, the Singapore-based hotel group, the hotel's exterior resembles a modern ski villa. Still, in its lavish interior, you'll find sushi restaurants, open fireplaces, and contemporary hotel room furnishings.

Although winter sports enthusiasts are the crowd that Chedi Andermatt caters to, the après-ski game is what it excels at. First, guests can make their way back to one of

119 lavish rooms after a day on the slopes, which are full of warm woodsy details and cozy lounge spots. Guests then choose the next pleasant space to visit, ranging from a quiet cigar lounge, a full-service bar furnished with plenty of leather sofas, or a Finnish barrel sauna and spa and indoor lap pool.

## 6. Gstaad Palace

### Key Specs:

- » Free Wi-Fi: Yes
- » Resort Fees: No
- » Room Rate: $$$$

**Notable Amenities:** Chauffeured Rolls-Royces, complimentary breakfast and restaurant credits daily, indoor-outdoor pool

**Address:** Palacestrasse 28, 3780 Gstaad, Switzerland

**Official Website:** https://www.palace.ch/en/

You can feel the majestic presence of Gstaad Palace even before stepping foot through the doors, like a fairytale castle nestled away in Berner Oberland, fully equipped with towers, turrets, and flags. First established in 1913, the hotel radiates history and luxury around every corner. Lounging and resting up are ideally provided by the hotel's rooms and suites, with curious details such as plaid wallpaper and decorative throw pillows. The "Cosy Room," the smallest option available, has its own seating area and an expansive bathroom and tub.

Regardless of its nearly imposing, luxurious design, Gstaad Palace is an excellent lodging option for families with children. The hotel holds kid-exclusive holiday parties and delightfully fun activities such as pony rides and baking lessons. In addition, one of the parks even has a bouncy castle. The Kids' Club is provided so parents can drop off their children and enjoy a few adult activities at the hotel. A few of these well worth trying are the massage from the Palace Spa and indulging in truffle fondue from the La Fromagerie underground.

# 7. Kulm Hotel

## Key Specs:

- » Free Wi-Fi: Yes
- » Resort Fees: No
- » Room Rate: $$$$

**Notable Amenities:** Reduced price ski passes, ice skating rink on-site, complimentary laundry service for children

**Address:** Via Veglia 18, 7500 St. Moritz, Switzerland

**Official Website:** https://www.kulm.com/en/#

At the time of its establishment in 1856, the Kulm Hotel became the first hotel in St. Moritz, the storied ski town. Many other accommodations are available in the region, yet the Kulm Hotel is one of the best. Certain perks remain unchanged—like the striking Alpine scenery and proximity to the primary ski funicular—but in the 21st century, a line of renovations has maintained the hotel's fresh and modern appeal. The 164 rooms are available in multiple sizes, ranging from comfortable single rooms to multi-bedroom suites featuring fireplaces and lake-view balconies.

However, the consistent lineup of activities is the primary attraction at Kulm Hotel. During the Winter Olympics of 1928 and 1948, the hotel hosted many events, so it adequately prepared for winter sports of all types. The concierge can help obtain reduced-price ski passes, book a thrilling bobsled run, or even arrange pickup outside the hotel by a horse-drawn carriage. The summer season also provides a plethora of fun, such as an on-site golf course, hiking trails, and lake watersports. Have an action-filled itinerary, then relax at Kulm Hotel's spa and Michelin-starred eateries.

# 8. Grand Hotel Kronenhof Pontresina

## Key Specs:

- » Free Wi-Fi: Yes
- » Resort Fees: No
- » Room Rate: $$$

**Notable Amenities:** Unlimited spa use, complimentary shuttle service, heated ski lockers

**Address:** Via Maistra 130, 7504 Pontresina, Switzerland

**Official Website:** https://www.kronenhof.com/en/#

Approximately five miles outside of St. Moritz, Pontresina is a beautiful mountain village ideal for travelers seeking something slightly more understated. This isn't to suggest that the town isn't any less extravagant than other Swiss ski towns—one prime example would be Grand Hotel Kronenhof Pontresina, a neo-Baroque resort that looks like it came out of a Wes Anderson film. Since 1848, the hotel has been taking in guests, and despite the sleek and modern appearances of the guest rooms, you can find gorgeous reminders of the past in the velvet-clad lounges and frescoed lobby.

Much like other Swiss hotels, Grand Hotel Kronenhof Pontresina is splendid in outdoor fun and après-ski lounging. Guests can partake in tobogganing, skiing, or going on a full-moon snowshoe tour. During the summer, the outdoor enjoyment switches to sailing, paragliding, mountain biking, and trekking with local mountain goats. (The hotel staff can assist in planning all of these outings and then some.) When the day comes to a close, amenities such as saunas, spa treatments, a glass-walled indoor pool, three restaurants, and a bowling alley serving made-to-order fondue are all accessible.

# 9. The Omnia

## Key Specs:

- » Free Wi-Fi: Yes
- » Resort Fees: No
- » Room Rate: $$$$

**Notable Amenities:** Train station transfers, balconies available in all rooms, complimentary breakfast

**Address:** Auf dem Fels, 3920 Zermatt, Switzerland

**Official Website:** https://www.the-omnia.com/en/hotel

Overlooking Zermatt and towering high on a rock, the Omnia combines modern American architecture and the traditional mountain lodge. After a glass elevator ascension constructed directly into the cliff, guests are greeted by a brightly-lit lobby and staff dressed in Marc Jacobs uniforms. Ali Tayar, a New York-based architect, was the mastermind behind the design of the 30 rooms and suites, with the spaces founded on clean lines, warm woods, and no clutter.

The Zen vibe stretches out to the spacious wellness center, where guests can relax in an indoor-outdoor pool, botanical-infused steam room, Finnish sauna, Turkish bath, and an outdoor whirlpool with scenic views of the Matterhorn. In addition, the hotel restaurant provides a tasting menu and à la carte dishes, utilizing vegetarian recipes and seasonal ingredients.

# 10. Grand Hotel Les Trois Rois

## Key Specs:

- » Free Wi-Fi: Yes
- » Resort Fees: No
- » Room Rate: $$$$

**Notable Amenities:** Complimentary non-alcohol minibars, cigar lounge, pet-friendly rooms

**Address:** Blumenrain 8, 4001 Basel, Switzerland

**Official Website:** https://www.lestroisrois.com/en

Contrary to many Swiss cities which are awash with five-star hotels, only one is located in Basel: a Belle Époque beauty on the Rhine banks, the Hotel Les Trois Rois was first established in 1844, but in 2006 it underwent an extensive renovation, bringing its glamour back to life. Currently, it remains one of the town's most desirable addresses. Covering every inch of space are subtle glimmers of old-school luxury, from the lobby adorned with crystalline chandeliers to marbled columns and the servers decked in tuxedos at Cheval Blanc, the hotel restaurant dishes out French haute cuisine.

Equally as remarkable are the 101 guest rooms, with thick curtains, darkly patterned wallpaper, and velvet-lined furniture. However, to experience more remarkable benefits, an upgrade to a suite is well worth it: the Napoleon Suite is lime-green and extra luxurious, with stucco work and ceiling frescoes. In addition, the

Rooftop Suite features three bathrooms, a roof terrace, and a hot tub. Everyday afternoon tea, a cigar lounge, and a fitness center with a river view offer additional amenities.

# Seasonal Outdoor Activities to Enjoy in Switzerland

## -Spring-

### 1. Hiking in the region of Jungfrau

- » **Suitable For:** Adventure, Photography
- » **Open From:** March–June

As a mountainous paradise in the springtime, the Jungfrau region is an excellent destination for outdoor exploration due to its extensive network of hiking trails. Gorgeous scenery of alpine vistas, emerald green slopes, tranquil blue lakes, and elegant flower fields can be admired from these trails, with snow-capped peaks as the perfect backdrop.

Grindelwald's Eiger Trail, Murren's Blumenthal, and Via Ferrata are all widely used hiking routes. However, explorers frequently detour from these trails to seek quieter routes such as Obersteinberg, which begins at the Stechelberg village. Signposts inform travelers that most tracks are navigable.

## 2. Whitewater rafting in Lütschine River

- » **Suitable For:** Adventure, Couples, Families
- » **Open From:** March–June

A few of Switzerland's best rivers have become adventurous hotspots for whitewater rafting lovers. Specifically, the Lütschine in the Bernese Oberland region is desirable as a thrilling sports destination. Slightly north of the Alps in Berne, the river rapids extend from Zweilütschinen to Lake Brienz.

As exciting class III-IV rapids, the waters here will take you on an exhilarating journey down the gorgeous Interlaken valley. Photo services are included with most rafting operators to capture the memories of your life moments along the river.

# -Summer-

## 1. Gelmer Funicular Sightseeing

- » **Suitable For:** Adventure, Photography, Couples, Families

» **Open From:** June, September, and October: daily from 9 a.m. to 4 p.m. July–August: daily from 9 a.m. to 5 p.m.
» **Address:** 3864 Guttannen, Switzerland

On a pleasant summer day in the Swiss countryside, a relaxing ride aboard the Gelmerbahn (Gelmer Funicular) is an excellent way to take in the scenic panoramas. Originally one of Europe's steepest funicular rides, it was once a means of transporting construction materials for the Gelmersee Dam in the 1920s.

Adrenaline junkies will love the particular thrill of riding down the mountain slopes inclined over 45°. In addition, 24 passengers may board the funicular at a time, and return ride tickets can be bought, starting at 32 Swiss Frances for adults and 12 Swiss Frances for children between 6 and 16 years old.

## 2. Paragliding at Lauterbrunnen

» **Suitable For:** Adventure, Photography
» **Open From:** July–August

You can soar high across the skies on a tandem paragliding adventure through the stunning Swiss countryside. Tandem flights are offered by various operators from the central town in the Jungfrau region known as Lauterbrunnen. Before taking off from a gentle slope, a few safety briefings and practice sessions will be conducted.

You and your pilot guide will fly high over the mountains and far-off meadows, then circle around to witness some of the most spectacular Alpine landscapes. You'll also get glimpses of the nearby mountain villages, typically hidden from view within the hills.

## 3. Jetboating in Interlaken

- » **Suitable For:** Adventure, Photography
- » **Open From:** 9 a.m. to 5 p.m. daily
- » **Address:** Am Quai, 3806 Bönigen, Switzerland

Perfect for thrill seekers and adrenaline junkies, guests can enjoy high-speed boating excitement on Interlaken's Lake Brienz. Up to 11 passengers can board jetboats as they share an exhilarating ride while the pilot guns the engines for speed runs, twisting turns, and complete 360° spins. This experience will be memorable as having plenty of wind in your hair and face spraying moments.

Guests will also pay a visit to the base of the tumbling Giessbach Waterfalls. Among the adrenalizing excitement, there's plenty of time to admire the stunning scenery of the turquoise lake surrounded by lush forests and the Swiss Alps as the backdrop.

## 4. Taking a ride down to Oeschinen Lake

- » **Suitable For:** Adventure, Photography, Families
- » **Open From:** May–October: daily from 9:30 a.m. to 4:30 p.m.
- » **Address:** 3718 Kandersteg, Switzerland

The Rodelbahn, also known as the Alpine Slider, is a thrilling summer toboggan ride down a purpose-built slide track that makes its way through the picturesque countryside looking down on Oeschinen Lake. You'll enjoy a comfortable ride sitting in a wheeled sled as you slide through the straights and curves over a 750-meter course.

Oeschinensee's cable car station is the starting point of the Alpine Slider, with summer exclusively being its open season and only in dry weather conditions. This highly addicting ride starts at 4 Swiss Frances for adults, while children ride for only 3 Swiss Frances.

# -Autumn-

## 1. Camping in Arolla

- » **Suitable For:** Adventure, Couples, Families
- » **Open From:** September–December
- » **Address:** Route de Tsallion, 1986 Evolène, Switzerland

Autumn is the season of nature's liveliest colors, and there's no better way to enjoy this scenic beauty than to spend a few nights camping in the stunning Swiss landscape. One of Switzerland's top-tier camping experiences is offered at the village of Arolla, one of the highest-altitude campgrounds in Europe.

The campground is nestled within lush pine tree forests, with Mount Collon's glacial peaks looming as a backdrop. The campground is located roughly 1,998 meters above sea level. Despite being in the heart of a lush landscape, the campground offers well-maintained, modern sanitary facilities and hot showering areas.

## 2. Mountain biking in Zermatt

- » **Suitable For:** Adventure, Couples, Families
- » **Open From:** September–December

Zermatt offers various thrilling and scenic mountain bike trails to venture around the surrounding area. Natural materials have constructed some of the courses here, which flow over the steep terrain, while others are built of manufactured materials. However, despite these differences in design, they all share the same captivating natural scenery.

To get a first glimpse of the mountain biking experience in the Alps, the Moos and Sunnegga trails offer a moderate biking experience. However, the Obere Kelle Trail challenges more experienced riders, featuring more difficult climbs interspersed with beautiful vistas.

# -Winter-

## 1. Skiing in the Alps

- » **Suitable For:** Adventure, Photography, Families, Luxury
- » **Open From:** January–February

The most desirable skiing hotspots in the Swiss Alps include Zermatt under the spectacular pyramid-shaped mountain of Matterhorn, along with the world's premium winter-sports resort known as St. Moritz. In addition, the link between Davos and Klosters, known as Parsenn, is also a winter lover's paradise with several skiing playgrounds.

Most of these Swiss ski resorts cater to a vast range of travelers thanks to a wide selection of facilities. Hardcore skiing experts can push their skills on challenging courses, while families and beginners can enjoy casual fun on gentle slopes.

## 2. Sledging from Preda to Bergün

- » **Suitable For:** Adventure, Photography
- » **Open From:** January–February

Travelers can embark on one of Switzerland's most popular sledging trackers by riding the Albula line of the Rhaetian Railway to Preda. Enjoying breathtaking Swiss scenery is one treat of this train ride, passing the Landwasser Viaduct and through a spiraling tunnel. This exhilarating 6-kilometer trail offers alpine sightseeing through viaducts as it twists and turns.

Riders seeking a more thrilling run can enjoy an exciting ride down to Darlux on a steep ski lift with hairpin turns.

# SWISS ARCHITECTURE

Despite the country's small size, Switzerland has an impressive amount of fine architecture. The beneficial location across significant trade routes and varied architectural traditions among the four national languages influences Switzerland's architecture. No specific indication is present among the most admirable buildings in Swiss architecture. Variety is the most intriguing and unique aspect of building design, spiced with simplicity, history, luxury, and traditions.

The variety in the country's architecture is very distinguishable by each geographical region. For example, the country's northern area is influenced by the Romans and Italians, the southern area is adorned with German style, and the French influenced the country's eastern regions.

Due to this regional variety, Switzerland has all the primary trends apparent in European architecture. In modern-day Switzerland, buildings of all significant architectural designs can be admired, including Gothic,

Roman, Renaissance, Modern, Postmodern, Baroque, and others.

Geneva, Basel, Sion, Chur, and Lausanne's cathedrals are where you can find the Romanesque style from the twelfth century. Not only does this style make a statement, but the lavishly rich expression is a feature of multiple castles and fortresses dotting the country. Until modern times, many of these were well-maintained and in good condition.

The Muenster (Münster) of Schaffhausen (12th century) is a prime example of church construction during the Romanesque period. A visual representation of Gothic architecture is Lausanne's Cathedral of Notre Dame, stylistically influenced by models of North France. Baroque architecture dominates in the Einsiedeln cloister and the Cathedral of St. Gall.

The vast diversity in the vernacular style is due to the significant isolation between villages within the Alpine mountain ranges and Jura Mountains, along with a difference in regional languages. Visually speaking, the styles of villages in each region differ due to varying traditions, different climate conditions, and the building materials used.

Representing only one of several traditional designs, the Swiss chalet style has remained popular since the nineteenth century. The original inspirations were the mountainous Alpine regions of Central Europe and Switzerland's rural chalets.

Coming from traditional building designs, the style is characterized by extensively projecting roofs and facades abundantly decorated with wooden balconies and carved ornaments. The style became more highly desired during the initial rushes of tourism of the rich from Northern and Western Europe. Because of this, the Swiss chalet style has spread through other European countries and North America.

Since Switzerland has remained a peaceful country for over 200 years, the Swiss people were able to preserve the structure of valuable and historic buildings, which tourists can still admire today.

Due to the implementation of historic preservation laws and tourism, several villages of varying sizes have maintained their historical core buildings. In addition, most of these have received recognition from UNESCO as "Cultural Heritage of Humanity," so Switzerland is often named an open-air museum.

# Famous Switzerland Landmarks

## 1. Bellinzona Castles

This historic town is found within Ticino, an Italian-speaking canton in Switzerland. This historic town features three castles, the best-preserved castles in the country—Montebello, Castelgrande, and Sasso Corbaro. Additionally, they have been nominated as a UNESCO World Heritage Site.

These three magnificent castles are some of the country's best-hidden gems, with fewer foreign tourists visiting here than other world-famous destinations, including Schilthorn and Zermatt. However, Bellinzona is a popular destination amongst many Swiss tourists from German-speaking cantons. They admire its enjoyable, unusual atmosphere and the southern charm drastically different from Switzerland's German and French-speaking regions.

These castles had long been a cause for dispute between the Swiss and Italians, who were in conflict over their control. As a result, to this day, the three castles have been collectively named the "Tre Castelli" and are commonly regarded as one of the Southern Alps' best fortification examples.

A minimum of half a day is required for visiting travelers to ensure enough time to tour the three castles and explore their museums. Travelers can enjoy additional sightseeing and a tasty lunch at Old Town Bellinzona after the tour. In addition, while taking a stroll along Viale Della Stazione, the city's busiest street, you will find several unique stores, small cafes, and restaurants.

Bellinzona is ideal for those traveling to Italy and passing through Switzerland. For travelers, it serves as an enjoyable getaway making their journey north to Switzerland or back the other way. The intersection of roads to San Bernardino, St. Gotthard, and Lucomagno passes is where the town is located. This intersection of streets is one of Southern Switzerland's most bustling thoroughfares.

## 2. Chapel Bridge in Lucerne

A highly desired landmark in Lucerne, Switzerland, is the Chapel Bridge, also known as Kapellbrücke, which got its name from the St. Peter's Chapel nearby. As one of Lucerne's most popular tourist attractions, this architectural masterpiece is distinguishable by its iconic covered design and wooden construction. Built in 1333, the early pedestrian bridge is rooted in historical significance. It was constructed over the Reuss River as a connector with the town's right and left side's new area. The purpose was to safeguard Lucerne from attacks coming from the south.

Tourists can find magnificent interior paintings from the 17th century at the historical Chapel Bridge. Unfortunately, a fire in 1993 destroyed two-thirds of the pictures, but a few were restored successfully. Included with the bridge is a water tower, which was once used as a prison. Now, it's a scenic attraction that stands on the water and supplements the bridge's beauty. Unfortunately, however, it is not accessible to the public.

The original length of the Chapel Bridge was approximately 200 meters at the time of its construction. However, as the years passed, multiple shortenings and replenishments of the river bank diminished its length to only 170 meters. Thankfully, since Lucerne is adequately connected to all of Switzerland's major cities, traveling to Chapel Bridge is accessible by train and road.

No entrance fee is required to access the bridge. However, from January to early February, the paintings are removed in place of modern carnival-themed pictures. Therefore, travelers cannot view historical paintings during this time.

## 3. Chillon Castle

Chillon Castle is believed to be one of Switzerland's most visited tourist sites. Its appearance is equally captivating, and located on a similarly beautiful small, rocky island in Lake Geneva. Not only is it visually appealing, but tourists can explore several rooms in its medieval interior.

Initially constructed in the 12th century, Chillon Castle has been continuously renovated. Today, over 400,000 tourists visit annually to admire the 14th-century wall paintings, parade halls, underground vaults, and the castle's bedroom, which has been preserved since its original construction dating back to the Bernese rule time.

Tourists can explore the castle by themselves, join a guided tour, or use an audio tour rental, which discloses information on the castle's various rooms. Other features of the castle include a dungeon/cellar, four grand halls, three courtyards, and a variety of rooms and stairwells. Several of these rooms were restored to their original glory many centuries ago.

At least a few hours will be required to explore all the castle's rooms. However, if you'd instead explore every nook and cranny of this historical beauty, half a day will suffice.

Avenue de Chillon 21, 1820 Veytaux is the address of the Chillon Castle and is easy to access by riding Bus 201 to the Chillon stop. Those who prefer a more scenic route can take the ferry crossing Lake Geneva to the Villeneuve Gare terminal. Open daily, the Chateau de Chillon is available for viewing from 9 a.m. to 7 p.m.

## 4. Gruyere Medieval Castle

Although the name "Gruyere" is typically associated with a type of delicious cheese by most people, Gruyere is much more than just cheese. Perched on the peak of an isolated hill and towering over the village below is the glorious medieval castle known as Gruyeres. Initially constructed in the 13th century by the Count of Gruyeres to maintain control over the local area, it became the home of multiple Counts of Gruyeres throughout the 13th and 16th centuries.

Custodians were granted residence in the castle between 1555 to 1798, then followed by administration leaders. The castle was then sold to the Balland and Bovy families in 1849. They then restored it and repurposed the castle as their summer home. The canton of Fribourg then bought back the castle in 1938 and converted it into a museum. Today, 800 years of the castle's history are showcased with unique collections of tapestries, historical furniture, paintings, towers, stained glass windows, gardens, and ramparts.

Development of the town took place beneath the castle, and today it is a charming cobblestoned, well-maintained village. Gruyeres was declared the most beautiful village in the French-speaking region of Switzerland in 2014.

A wide array of fascinating things to see and do is part of the Gruyeres touring experience, along with the medieval village and castle. Located on the opposite side of the railway station is the cheese factory 'La Maison Du Gruyere,' which features an exciting and entertaining tour that allows guests to watch the cheese-making process and shows the history of cheese in the region. Within proximity is the large Maison Cailler chocolate factory, where a fantastic tour and tasting are also available.

From Geneva, Zurich, and Montreux is about an enjoyable two-hour train ride from Gruyeres. If you're planning a trip to Gruyeres, some local specialties make the experience worthwhile. The traditional fondue made of Fribourg cheese, the decadent meringues with double cream, and the luxurious taste of chocolate are a few of the delicious treats from the Gruyeres district.

## 5. Jet D'eau Geneva

A highly iconic landmark in the gorgeous Swiss city of Geneva is the Jet d'Eau (or "water jet" if directly translated from French). It is one of the tallest fountains worldwide, standing 140 meters high, and since 1891, it has been a symbol of Geneva.

Initially, the fountain was constructed as a relief valve for pipes as they supplied water jewelry makers of the city. Equivalent to 500 liters a second of lake water, it shoots up 200 kilometers per hour above Lake Geneva. The fountain symbolizes Geneva's vitality and status on an international level.

The Jet d'Eau water fountain can be found in the Geneva Harbor or "La Rade," on the left bank just slightly off Eaux-Vives. The fountain is visible from most of the city's viewpoints while coming in to touch down at the airport. Often lit up at night, the fountain is an iconic aspect of Geneva's skyline. The most spectacular view, however, can be witnessed at the Bains des Paquis, where tourists can capture a fantastic selfie with the water fountain.

The fountain does not run throughout the year and is periodically off limits for maintenance, and remains turned off at night when winds are strong and the temperatures drop below zero degrees.

## 6. Lavaux Vineyard Terraces

Spanning nearly 30 kilometers of lower slopes in the Swiss mountainside along Lake Geneva's shores is the Lavaux Vineyard Terraces, from Chateau de Chillon to the eastern fringes of Laussane in the region of Vaud.

While some evidence exists that the region's vines were planted during the Roman times, today's vine terraces are traceable to the 11th century—when the Benedictine and Cistercian monasteries dominated the area. The Lavaux Vineyard Terraces are an outstanding example of the relationship between the climate and the region's inhabitants over several centuries. It is designed to utilize local resources to the maximum to produce a highly regarded wine, which has always maintained economic importance.

The Lavaux vineyard landscape is a marvel of ingenuity—it displays the results of contact between people and their climate over the centuries distinctly and fruitfully.

A highly appreciated, superior wine results from fully optimized local resources, becoming a staple of the local economy. In response to rapid urban development over recent decades, local communities pushed security initiatives firmly. As a result, the vineyards are safeguarded today as world heritage and accessible for later generations to marvel at and explore through the premises.

There are great places to explore in the vineyards, and the best way to do so is by bike on a warm day filled with sunshine. Pack a picnic lunch, or visit one of several taverns along the way for the ultimate enjoyment.

# 7. Mount Pilatus

Bordering Lucerne, Switzerland, Mount Pilatus has various features that make it incredibly iconic. For starters, since 1889, when the machinery was initially displayed at the Paris World Fair, the steepest cogwheel railway scales the 48% gradient mountainside. The beginning of the 40-minute railway ride is in Alpnachstad, ending at Pilatus Kulm, the highest point of Mount Pilatus. You can instead ride a gondola, followed by an aerial cableway, back and forth between Kriens to Pilatus Kulm. Combination and single-way tickets are both available.

Travelers are welcome to venture into the regions at scheduled intermediate stops with several fun activities. For example, you can hike, partake in a glider ride, take a ropes course, and rest at a playground with your family during the warmer months. Another spectacular activity not worth missing out on is the longest toboggan course in Fräkmüntegg, Switzerland, which measures 1,350 meters (0.8 miles). In winter, travelers can also indulge in sledding or snowshoeing beneath the gondola pathway at Fräkmüntegg or Krienseregg.

An additional cost is required for each activity. Tourists on a budget can expect to spend $9 per person for the toboggan run, which is an $80 savings for the dual experience of traversing the cogwheel railway to Pilatus Kulm and the back-down trip to Kriens by aerial cableway/gondola.

What also makes Mount Pilatus so iconic is the Middle Ages myths regarding the dragons that once inhabited the deep cracks of Pilatus. Traveling along the Dragon Trail to explore the area and take breaks to enjoy beautiful sightseeing is a must-try when visiting.

At the peak of Mount Pilatus, facilities are found within the hotel. Constructed in 1890, the hotel boasts glorious views of the nearby mountains. Indulge in delicious cuisine while watching paragliders take off from the top of Mount Pilatus.

# 8. Mount Titlis

A complete package deal can be enjoyed on an excursion to Mount Titlis, featuring a stunning glacier, panoramic scenery over snowy Alpine landscapes, an exhilarating cliff walk, and a ride on the first revolving aerial cableway worldwide.

Found in the heart of Switzerland and one of the region's most significant highlights, Mount Titlis stands at a mighty 3,020 meters and is endlessly covered in snow. In addition, to being a highly desired tourist destination, it is the only easily accessible glacier within the region.

The town of Engelberg provides access to Mount Titlis through a series of cable cars. Travelers will take a ride through Trübsee on the first one, a gorgeous Alpine lake where you can stop to go boat rowing and marvel at the scenic environment. The next leg to the mountain summit is on the prominent rotating cable car, the Titlis Rotair. As you journey up the mountain, the rotating cable car enables you to take in the scenic, snowy landscapes all around you.

Thanks to superb Swiss engineering, five levels are featured in the summer with many activities to try. The top level has the best of these activities, where grand viewing platforms allow you to enjoy the panoramic displays and have fun in the snow, even during summer. In addition, Europe's tallest suspension footbridge, the Titlis Cliff Walk, is found here. Looming several hundred meters over the glaciers below, walking across this bridge is an adrenalizing experience and is less scary than it sounds.

Another fantastic feature of Mount Titlis is the Glacier Cave constructed several meters beneath the glacier. Visiting this cave is truly an exciting experience thanks to sub-zero temperatures in the cave's interior, ice walls all around, and the fact that this location's ice is over

5,000 years old. Travelers should bundle up since it's winter at the summit year-round.

Even though it's an occasionally crowded, popular tourist destination, Mount Titlis is a phenomenal place to visit on a bucket list. To avoid dealing with crowds, the earlier you arrive, the better.

## 9. Rhine Falls

Located at Schaffhausen, the Rhine Falls is Europe's most massive plain waterfall and a must-see landmark for nature lovers in Switzerland. Visitor areas are on the Northern and Southern sides of the Rhine Falls. However, visiting both sides is advised to truly appreciate their splendor from all angles. This is possible thanks to an easy 3.4 km circular hike.

Laufen Castle, towering high above Rhine Falls, dominates the Southern Bank. There is a trail beginning from the castle, leading to multiple viewing platforms that lead you almost within arm's reach to the cascading water. The viewing platform ticket also allows tourists to visit the castle. Dominating the Northern bank is a smaller castle-like structure known as Schlössli Wörth, where the boat rides set off. With varying options, one allows you to stand on the rock in the center of the falls.

Visitation is free to the Rhine Fall's Northern bank, where most restaurants and souvenir shops are located. A picnic area with a waterfall view is also available.

Travelers who do the circular hike will be taken over the train bridge that crosses the river slightly over the falls. Stopping at Laufen Castle, the train is an ideal transportation option to consider if you're traveling from Zurich, which is slightly under 50 km away. Also possible is a combination trip to the Rhine Falls and a visit to Lake Constance or Stein am Rhein, a beautiful medieval village slightly further along the river.

## 10. Schilthorn-Piz Gloria

Among the tallest peaks in the Swiss Alps, Schilthorn-Piz Gloria towers at a staggering 2,070 meters/9,744 feet high and is famously recognized as a James Bond filming setting, making an appearance in the movie "On Her Majesty's Secret Service" in 1969.

Displayed proudly on the summit, the remarkable metal structure is home to a restaurant that rotates 360 degrees, a Hall of Fame exhibit of James Bond, and a substantial indoor cinema that shows re-runs of action scenes from the unforgettable Bond film. Schilthorn-Piz Gloria is worthy of a visit, even for those who aren't fans of James Bond.

Travelers can spot a platform outside the summit house with stunning panoramic visuals of three of Switzerland's tallest peaks: Eiger, Mönch, and Jungfrau, along with multiple hiking trails and adventure activities, such as a Via Ferrata (mountain-climbing). Suppose the activities aren't of much interest. In that case, you can just marvel at the captivating scenery or partake in the James Bond-themed champagne brunch experience within the rotating restaurant, which takes place every day until 2:00 p.m.

Interlaken is the closest town to Schilthorn-Piz Gloria. You can ride a bus from Interlaken to Stechelberg to access the summit. In addition, if you have vehicle access, you may also drive to Stechelberg, and the path is beautifully scenic and lined with gorgeous waterfalls. Stechelberg station provides paid parking access.

Starting at Stechelberg, the picturesque adventure up the mountain begins with boarding the first of four aerial cableways: Stechelberg, Gimmelwald, Mürren, Birg, and Schilthorn. Unique outlooks and stops along the way at a few beautiful villages are part of the cable car experience.

Arriving at the summit requires an approximately 40-minute-long journey. If time isn't a concern, travelers may also stop at one of the lovely mountain villages. From Gimmelwald or Mürren, the downward journey back to Stechelberg will lead you through some great green pastures and grazing livestock animals, an experience you must not miss out on.

An additional attraction to visit at Schilthorn is the adrenalizing Skyline Walk and Thrill Walk found at Birg cableway station. Travelers here can embark on a 200-meter walk along a transparent cliff-side pathway with glass flooring and sheer drop-offs.

Schilthorn-Piz Gloria cableway tickets cost approximately 108 Swiss francs for adults, and children can get in for 54 Swiss francs. Hiking, however, is free of charge.

## 11. Schäfler Ridge

Travelers can take one of Switzerland's most scenic hikes by hiking up Schäfler Ridge in the Ebenalp at 1,920 meters. As long as the weather is pleasant and clear, you may simultaneously overlook Austria and Germany from this stunning ridgeline.

Wasserauen is the hike's starting point, where travelers can choose between two options. The first would be a direct hike up to Schäfler. As such, the distance to hike is approximately 7.5 kilometers with an incline of 1,200 meters, which takes 3 to 4 hours to complete.

Thanks to the cable car station in Wasserauen, the most straightforward option is to travel by cable car up to Ebenalp and begin a hike there. A one-way trip on the cable car costs 20 Swiss francs (31 Swiss francs in return), but as a result, a 3-kilometer hike with approximately a 300-meter incline is all that's required to reach Schäfler ridge.

Upon arrival at Schäfler, a guesthouse will be spotted on top where travelers can recharge with snacks and drinks. Overnight stay in the guesthouse is also an option for those who want to view the sunrise or sunset from the top. However, booking your place ahead of time is recommended since it can fill up quickly.

Tourists can visit various other fascinating places in the Ebenalp region, which you can combine with the Schäfler ridge hike. Among Switzerland's most famous mountain huts is Berggasthaus Aescher, which is only a slight detour to visit even if you ride up the cable car. For a direct hike down to Schäfler, traversing on a hiking trail that travels through Seealpsee before reaching the parking lot is well worth it. However, despite being a highly scenic path, it's not recommended for beginners or individuals uncomfortable with heights.

## 12. Sphinx Observatory at Jungfraujoch

Among the top famous landmarks in Switzerland, Jungfraujoch is synonymous with the phrase "top of Europe." As a saddle within the Bernese Alps since 1912 and between the Jungfrau and Mönch peaks, this spot has been visited by travelers along the well-known Jungfrau rack railway line from Kleine Scheidegg.

A remarkable accomplishment of alpine construction is the railway line to Jungfraujoch.

Lying primarily in the Jungfrau Tunnel, it travels through the solid rock of the Eiger and Mönch mountains, ending at Europe's highest railway station known as Jungfraujoch station. However, considering the station itself is buried below the ground, the Sphinx Observatory is the most distinctive image of Jungfraujoch.

Perched above the station on a rocky ridge, the Sphinx Observatory is one of the highest astronomical observatories worldwide. In addition to a scientific observatory, an outdoor observation deck is available to the public and is Switzerland's second highest. It is accessible by an elevator from Jungfraujoch station, including a complex housing several restaurants and a post office.

A day trip along the Jungfrau railway is the ideal way to visit Jungfraujoch, either from Interlaken or Grindelwald or Lauterbrunnen's smaller mountain villages. Each leg of the journey may be covered by purchasing ticket packages, along with entry into Jungfraujoch. Blanketed in snow throughout the year, a clear day is an ideal time to visit to fully immerse yourself in the breathtaking vistas of the nearby mountains. Also accessible is an ice palace, an area for snow playing, and the opportunity to hike along the adjacent glacier.

## 13. St. Peterskirche in Zurich

Recognized worldwide as the birthplace of quality timepieces, it's no surprise that Europe's grandest clock face is located in Switzerland and is a must-see while visiting Zurich.

Located in the middle of St. Peterhofstatt and constructed on the Roman castle ruins next to Lindenhof Hill, St. Peterskirche is Zurich's longest-standing church. Here built during the 13th century, the miniature and earliest version of the church has long since had many additions made until the 16th century (the current structure). However, staying true to its origins, St. Peterskirche's foundations date back to the 9th century.

The 64-meter tall St. Peterskirche clock tower was intended as a watchtower and lookout post to alert the city of fires from 1340 until 1911. Built from over 40,000 shingles, the spire-decorated pitched roof is believed to be Zurich's only wooden roof.

As a national icon of Switzerland, the St. Peterskirche tower proudly boasts Europe's most enormous clock face. Grand medieval clock faces are on each of the tower's four sides, which have displayed the time since the 13th century. St. Peterskirche remained Zurich's official local time which accurately set all other clocks.

An impressive diameter of 8.64 meters is the measurement of each clock face, while the minute hands reach 5.73 meters and the hour hands measure 5.07 meters. Originating back to 1880 are five bells inside the clock tower, with the largest weight at 6 tonnes.

A visit to Quaibrüke (Quay Bridge) above the Limmat River is one of the top destinations to photograph Quaibrüke (Quay Bridge) to capture the magnificent clock faces along with the Fraumünster and

Grossmünster twin domes, which are beautiful landmarks of Zurich.

## 14. The Abbey of St. Gall

Situated in Switzerland's north-eastern region in St. Gall town, the Abbey of St. Gall's current design is primarily due to building campaigns of the 18th century.

Along with an incredible architectural ensemble, it features multiple buildings nestled together around Abbey central square: the west side's current cathedral, known as the medieval abbey church, alongside two towers and the ancient cloister that is now home to the glorious abbey library; the new canton authorities seat is known as the 'Neue Pfalz,' which is located on the east side. Among Switzerland's top famous landmarks, St. Gall's Abbey is more than just a fine example of a grand Carolingian monastery; it is also among the most important cultural centers in Europe, beginning in the 8th century until 1805 secularization.

In addition, it reflects monastic architectural tradition for 1200 years and serves as a traditional and exemplary ensemble of an expansive Benedictine monastery. The majority of significant architectural periods, ranging from the High Middle Ages to historicism, are displayed and protected in an exemplary fashion. Regardless of the various styles, the impression of overall unity is created by the humanist ensemble, surrounded on the north and west by primarily intact buildings of St. Gall city.

The High Baroque Library is among the most magnificent portrayals of its time, and the current cathedral is among the last notable constructions of Baroque abbey churches in the west. Along with the architectural context, the immeasurable cultural merits preserved at the Abbey are of distinct significance. In particular, the 7th and 8th-century Irish manuscripts and the 9th and 11th-century Medieval manuscripts of the St. Gall School documents concerning the background of the origins of Alemannic Switzerland and Caroline-era convent architecture.

Incredibly beautiful and currently protected as UNESCO World Heritage, it is among Europe's most famous monasteries.

## 15. The First Cliff Walk in Grindelwald

With a 45-meter suspension out from the cliffs, The First Cliff Walk is an engineering phenomenon that allows visitors to experience a suspended bird's eye view from this elevated platform. Using only a single rope system for its construction, the metal structure suspends the bridge from the face of the rock, with September 2015 being the time it was opened.

At Grindelwald First, it was the start of several captivating tourist attractions to open. The First Flyer and First Glider are also two exciting rides to experience.

Considering you can see the plunging cliff faces underneath your feet, The First Cliff Walk itself is slightly unsettling, but this once-in-a-lifetime experience is well worth it. Take in the beauty of the glorious Swiss mountains, surging waterfalls, and the emerald green valley below as a truly extraordinary moment.

Considering the everchanging mountain climate, it is essential to wear multiple layers and bring a jacket, regardless of what the weather in the village seems like that day. Even in the heart of the summer season, temperatures can rapidly plummet and become very frigid. However, depending on your energy reserves, getting to the First Cliff Walk is straightforward, with the Grindelwald First gondola being the easiest method of arrival. With a whisk from the Grindelwald village, you head straight to the top station of First.

A hike to the First Station is easy to tackle if you are physically fit and in good health. This is a physically demanding uphill climb from Grindelwald one way but provides extraordinary views along the trip.

Another fantastic walk is a trip to one of the most breathtaking high-altitude lakes known as Lake Bachalpsee; getting there in just a one-hour return from First Station.

## 16. The Lion Monument in Lucerne

As one of Lucerne's most prominent landmarks, the Lion Monument serves as a memorial dedicated to the 1,000 Swiss guards who died on August 10, 1792, in Paris while defending the life of King Louis XVI amid the French Revolution.

Annually, over a million tourists pay a visit to see this stone-carved imposing lion. A Swiss Guard named Karl Pfyffer was the man behind the vision of building this memorial, who fatefully was on leave visiting his Lucerne home on the same day of the tragedy. After returning home to Lucerne and years of service abroad, Pfyffer dedicated himself to constructing a monument to recognize those comrades in arms who perished in combat.

However, many years later, his vision came to be realized when his fundraising initiative financially covered the project. At that point, Bertel Thorvaldsen, a famous Danish artist, brought forth the grand model of a larger-than-life lion.

The reminder of this devastating tragedy in history is symbolized by the dying lion constructed inside a low cliff with water and trees surrounding it. Found in the heart of Lucerne, the Lion Monument is only a few steps from Lucerne Lake. Alongside it is the Glacier Garden of Lucerne and the Alpine Museum. Visiting the Lion Monument is free of charge.

## 17. The Glacier Express Trainline

The Glacier Express Trainline is more than just an iconic landmark—it's also the link between various other far-out landmarks that are otherwise not easy to access in the

Swiss Alps. Mountain passes, famous peaks, and UNESCO World Heritage Sites are connecting points.

The route's starting point is in Zermatt, a mountain resort just underneath the famous Matterhorn's peak, which inspired the Toblerone chocolate bar's pyramid shape. Reaching St. Moritz and the Piz Bernina is a 7–8 hour express train ride to the tallest mountain of the Eastern Alps. Widely regarded as the world's slowest fast train, the Glacier Express train is designed as a high-speed train, but it cannot reach high speeds for most of the journey due to the mountainous terrain.

The crossing at the UNESCO World Heritage Site, Landwasser Viaduct, is the line's most famous scene, which was constructed in 1901 as a single-track, six-arched railway viaduct of curved limestone. However, there are plenty of additional sites along this route, including 291 bridges and 91 tunnels dotting the 291-kilometer railway line. In addition, there are many other highlights to see, including the highest peak at Oberalp Pass and the Rhine Gorge, the River Rhine's source marker.

Individually booking the train ride can be done by visiting the Glacier Express. However, it is also part of local train passes and requires advanced booking with the Eurail/Interrail passes.

## 18. The Matterhorn

The Matterhorn, the triangular-shaped mountain peak towers above the Zermatt alpine village, is among Switzerland's most iconic landmarks. Although it is not the country's high peak at 4,478 meters, it is one of the most distinguishable by its shape.

Unfortunately, when travelers first climbed the Matterhorn in 1865, four of the six climbers fell to their deaths while descending. This tragedy brought worldwide recognition to the Matterhorn and has since attracted both climbers and non-climbers by the thousands.

For tourists not climbing the iconic peak, it's possible to take one of three Zermatt excursions to get incredible close-up views. Matterhorn Glacier Paradise (which also offers skiing year-round) and Rothorn are both accessible via cable car, while a cogwheel train reaches Gornergrat. All excursions offer stunning visuals of the Matterhorn, and taking one of these excursions is considered one of Zermatt's top activities.

Although regarded as a Swiss landmark, the Matterhorn borders the Switzerland and Italy border, and it is possible to ski on the border during the winter season. However, one of the most memorable moments of visiting the Matterhorn is during the sunrise when it's bathed in breathtaking orange colors.

The journey to visit the Matterhorn begins by traveling to the car-free village of Zermatt. Zermatt is the connecting point to regular train services operating all over Switzerland. For tourists arriving by car, a spacious public car park is found in the lower village of Tasch with train routes to Zermatt.

# Switzerland
# Flora & Fauna

In the miniature landscape of Switzerland, there are many plants and animals due to the vastly contrasting climates and altitudes. For example, travelers can find palm, cypress, almond, and orange trees throughout the lowlands. At a higher elevation of around 1,200 meters, maple, beech, and oak trees dot the landscape. At the elevated height of 1,700 meters, fir and pine trees dominate. Dwarf pines and larches will surprise you with their presence at 2,130 meters. And beyond the snow line, roughly one hundred species of plants make their home in the high altitudes, including the notable Edelweiss, the symbol of Switzerland.

The Edelweiss, also called Leontopodium alpinum, is a dearly cherished flower in Switzerland. It has long been an important symbol of Swiss folklore and grows in the Alps' highest altitudes. Since the 19th century, the Edelweiss has been distinguished by the snowy mountains' clarity. As time progressed, it evolved into a symbol of loyalty and true love, as several young men put their lives in jeopardy, gathering Edelweiss for their loved ones by scaling the mountaintops.

The Alpine flora's vibrant beauty and subtle color patterns are genuinely remarkable and must be seen in person to truly appreciate its glorious scenery. In addition, the climatic conditions drastically vary here, where temperature variations can differ more than 40°C between day and night.

The same degree of flora variety is also the case of Switzerland's native animal species; this includes 40,000 types such as deer, fox, boar, otter, chamois, and several others.

The Federal Act protects these florae and fauna through the Protection of Nature and Cultural Heritage, which encourages biodiversity preservation. In Switzerland, roughly 72 native plant and animal species are listed as threatened. Also playing a significant role in this biodiversity preservation and protection is the Swiss National Park. This territory is an extensive 170 km², along with most of the alpine landscape. Yet, the nature within these boundaries remains untouched.

Even today, on a few of the Alpine summits, several more plant species grow than there were up to a century ago. However, throughout this period, certain species have died out completely.

Among these wild animals that are considered endangered are the ptarmigan and mountain hare. Contributing to this threat is prolonged global warming because forests need a long time to adapt to these hotter conditions and may lack a timely response as the climate changes. However, only some in Switzerland are doomed to be lost. As a result, many people and organizations have dedicated themselves to preserving Switzerland's incredible plant and animal species from the threat of going extinct.

The country is still the origin of some of the most stunning, untouched mountain and valley territories worldwide. The lakes are prosperous with fish, and the mountains grow rich with vegetation. A trip to Switzerland will undoubtedly introduce its tourists to the astonishing, vast variety of landscapes, weather and climate conditions, and an abundance of plants and animals. Switzerland will captivate nature lovers with its unique charm as pristine forests, alluring Alpine landscapes, glossy rivers and lakes, and amazing animals and birds surround them.

# Switzerland's Best Zoos and Aquariums

## Zoo Zurich

**Recommended Duration:** 5 hours, 30 minutes

**Hours:** Daily 9 a.m.–5 p.m.

**Address:** Zürichbergstrasse 221, 8044 Zürich, Switzerland

**Price Range:** $$

**Parking Access:** Lot parking available

**Official Website:** https://www.zoo.ch/en

Zoo Zurich is a lush greenery oasis settled on a wooded hill east of downtown Zurich. Over 2,000 animals from approximately 250 different species are housed here. Along with a grand aquarium and open-aired aviary, the park has dedicated designated areas to animals of Africa, along with spacious enclosures for red pandas, tigers, lions, snow leopards, and otters. The zoo's most prominent tropical rainforest replica attraction offers visitors a hands-on learning experience about Madagascar's natural environments. In addition, with well-thought-out timing, visitors may be able to watch the daily penguin parade.

## Falconeria Locarno

**Recommended Duration:** 1 hour, 30 minutes

**Hours:** Open Saturday–Sunday, 12 p.m.–4 p.m. closed on weekdays

**Address:** Via delle Scuole 12, 6600 Locarno, Switzerland

**Price Range:** $$

**Parking Access:** Lot parking available

**Official Website:** https://falconeria.ch/?%2Fhistory

At Falconeria Locarno, visitors can expand their knowledge of the ancient practice of falconry and view live demonstrations. Dating back 4,000 years ago across the Asian plains, this method of hunting was initially introduced to Europe by Emperor Frederick II of Hohenstaufen after embarking on a trip to Arabia. Above and before your eyes, you can marvel as falcons, vultures, owls, eagles, and other prey birds perform majestic acrobatic flights. Visitors can listen to commentary on each bird species' unique characteristics, along with falconry's origins, during the show. However, this commentary is only offered in German and Italian. There is plenty to do between shows, such as checking out the aviaries, picking up a snack, conversing with the falconers, or exploring the grounds.

## Zoo Basel

**Recommended Duration:** 1 hour, 30 minutes

**Hours:** Open daily 8 a.m.–5:30 p.m.

**Address:** Binningerstrasse 40, 4054 Basel, Switzerland

**Price Range:** $$

**Parking Access:** Limited parking spaces

**Official Website:** https://www.zoobasel.ch/en/

For a wide range of animals of various sizes, take a trip to Zoo Basel, where endangered species have been bred in captivity as a feature of the zoo's renowned program. Initially constructed in 1874, the zoo brings in almost 2 million visitors annually. It has land coverage of approximately 11 hectares (26 acres) in a municipal setting and a short walk to downtown Basel. Five thousand animals reside here, including rhinoceroses, penguins, pygmy hippopotamuses, squirrel monkeys, snow leopards, European otters, and cheetahs.

# Aquatis Aquarium-Vivarium Lausanne

**Recommended Duration:** 2 hours, 30 minutes

**Hours:** Open daily 10 a.m.–6 p.m.

**Address:** Rte de Berne 144, 1010 Lausanne, Switzerland

**Parking Access:** Lot parking available

**Official Website:** https://www.aquatis.ch/en/

Located in Lausanne, Switzerland, the Aquatis Aquarium is an exciting and interesting tourist attraction and Europe's largest freshwater aquarium. It officially opened on October 21, 2017, and is roughly 15 minutes from the city center. Over 10,000 freshwater fish and various reptile and amphibian species make their home at Aquatis. Originating from 5 continents worldwide, Aquatis is dedicated to promoting and protecting these animals.

While walking on the grounds and through the aquariums, visitors will discover the rivers and lakes of Asia, Africa, and the Amazonian region. A wide array of projections, lights, mirrors, and information displays enhance the experience while walking through the aquarium, with most visitors typically spending an hour minimum here. Although likely fearsome to younger children, older children may enjoy the moving crocodile exhibits at Aquatis Aquarium. The information screens at each station provide educational information in English, German, and French about the animals in each display.

## Tierpark Bern

**Recommended Duration:** 1 hour, 30 minutes

**Hours:** Open daily 9 a.m.–4:30 p.m.

**Address:** Tierparkweg 1, 3005 Bern, Switzerland

**Parking Access:** Lot parking available

**Official Website:** https://tierpark-bern.ch/

As a public zoo based in Bern, Switzerland, it was first established in 1937 and operated by Tierparkverein Bern, an affiliated association. Bern city is the park's proprietary and brings forth most of the financing. Nestled in the Dählhölzli forest and situated on the Aare river bank close to the historical city center, the zoo has around 3,000 animals on exhibit and employs a staff crew of 27. This zoo is a highly desirable family destination thanks to the Kinderzoo, Eulen Bistro, spacious forest playground, and being open 365 days a year. Some magnificent animals displayed at Tierpark Bern are leopards, bears, seals, wolves, musk oxen, eagle owls, monkeys, and gophers.

## Natur- und Tierpark Goldau

**Recommended Duration:** 2 hours, 30 minutes

**Hours:** Daily 9 a.m.–5 p.m.

**Address:** Parkstrasse 40, 6410 Goldau, Switzerland

**Price Range:** $$$

**Parking Access:** Lot parking available

**Official Website:** https://www.tierpark.ch/

One of six scientifically managed zoos in Switzerland, Natur- und Tierpark Goldau is situated in the region tragically impacted by the 1806 Goldau landslide. Visitors can spend time with and feed fallow deer, sika deer, and mouflons in the spacious, freely walkable park. An addition to the European Endangered Species Programme, rare mammal and bird species are reared by the park, such as European bison, Syrian brown bears, and Northern bald ibises. Particularly noteworthy is the international species program dedicated to bearded vultures. Natur- und Tierpark Goldau operates a school within the park in which zoo pedagogues and park rangers provide school class workshops, guided tours for schools, and visitor groups to the animals.

For example, park rangers offer commentated feedings of bears, wild boars, and cormorants and assistance as informants to individual visitors while on a walkabout. Recently, the animal park surface has been expanded from 17 to 34 hectares. In addition to the original forest and lake within the park, there is newly added land on the other side of the road. A 70-meter-wide wildlife crossing allows visitors to bridge the road, which was the first expansion stage's main feature.

At the foot of the Rossberg mountain in the Grosswiyer area, the park opened a spacious site for brown bears and grey wolves. The other expansion plans included vivariums, beaver lodges, a Phasianidae site, an amphibian biotope, and a rare domestic animal farm. In addition, a once artificial creek bed has been revitalized and restored, which allows a "reconquest" of the stretch of water by the Grosswiyer park area's flora and fauna.

# Best Traditional Events in Switzerland

## 1. Basel Carnival

**Location:** Basel, Basel Region

**Months of Operation:** February/March

Following Ash Wednesday, Monday to Thursday, the Fasnacht (carnival) of Basel is recognized as Switzerland's grandest, most notable festival, with around 15,000 to 20,000 masked participants celebrating the event.

On the Monday following Ash Wednesday, the intro is the Morgestraich. As four in the morning strikes the clock, fifers and drummers adorned in charivari costumes and masks with miniature headlights gather in groups. They go through the town's dark center while playing carnival tunes. Carnival cliques, also known as the Cliquen, carry see-through lanterns designed from wood and canvas. Most of these reach over an impressive three meters (nine feet) high. The light from these lanterns illuminates the carved-out silhouette of an event marked by the previous year. The marches played are famous tunes from past decades, with new ones added periodically.

On Monday and Wednesday afternoons, the Cliquen march through the city on a planned route, making their way through crowds of spectators. In the months leading up to Fasnacht, a new theme is chosen and transposed to the masks, lanterns, and costumes. It's also displayed on the leaflets distributed amongst the spectators, written in Basel dialect in prose and verse. Individuals and small groups pay a visit from bar to bar on both evenings, portraying events of the past year through song and acting. They are all equipped with witty remarks like the caricatures or Schnitzelbängg. Tuesday evening is devoted to the masked musicians, also known as the Guggemuusige, who make their presence in the city streets with their improvised cacophony.

To several individuals, the Gässle, or wandering through the tapered alleyways, is the best part of the event. Roaming through the old city's streets, masked groups and individuals play drums and pipes, with marching spectators following behind them. These festivities commence until Thursday at four o'clock in the morning. Then another year must pass until the clock strikes four again on the following Ash Wednesday, ringing in Basel's next, much-anticipated carnival.

## 2. Sechseläuten

**Location:** Zurich

**Months of Operation:** Mid-Late April

This spring-season tradition in Zurich received its strange name from the medieval practice of ringing a bell of the Grossmünster at six o'clock every evening to declare the working day's end during the summer semester. Since it marked springtime's beginning, the bell's first ringing provided the ideal opportunity for celebration.

A new primary protagonist, Böögg, was included in the festivities in the 19th century. This figure resembles a snowman, symbolizes winter, and is stuffed with firecrackers. It is set ablaze when the clock of the Grossmünster church reaches 6 p.m. to forecast the coming summer's weather. So naturally, the quicker the explosion of the figurehead, the better the summer weather will be. In addition to guild members adorned in historical costumes, the festival is denoted by music ensembles, flowers, flags, and horses.

## 3. Finale Nationale de la Race d'Hérens

**Location:** Aproz, Valais

**Months of Operation:** Early May

Cow fights commence all across the region where the Hérens breed has its home (Central Valais, Valle d'Aosta in Northern Italy). More than all other breeds, these miniature black cows with stubby durable horns have maintained the instinct to organize themselves to form a social hierarchy. Finally, beginning in early spring, in a usually fierce competition, the queen cow who will lead the herd up to the Alpine meadows is declared.

The nature of fights occurs spontaneously rather than in an organized way; simply put, each cow decides on her opponent in the spur of the moment. She abruptly stops grazing, lowers her head, snorts, and rakes the ground with her hooves. If a cow of similar toughness welcomes the challenge, time is well-spent in greeting her opponent the same way.

They approach each other hesitantly, and the fight begins. With the clashing of heads and locking of horns, each cow tries to manage a solid hold. They then stand firmly, trying to push the other back with all their might. Outperformed by overwhelming strength, the weaker cow is forced to retreat. The winning cow establishes dominance by adding more jabs with her horns after the loser turns around and flees.

Along with these random battles, there are also organized competitions to decide on a cantonal and regional queen.

# 4. Swiss Yodeling Festival

**Location:** Varies

**Months of Operation:** June

Natural yodeling exists worldwide but is more prominent in mountainous and difficult-to-access terrains where the technique was intended for communication over far stretching distances. Although yodeling most likely lived during the Stone Age, the 19th century is when choir singing recently developed.

Swiss Yodeling is one of the most widespread and unforgettable of Switzerland's long list of traditional events. Held once every three years in varying locations, visitors will encounter numerous concerts, folkloric exhibitions, and traditional Swiss cuisine.

# 5. International Alphorn Festival

**Location:** Nendaz, Valais

**Months of Operation:** Late July

Historically, the alphorn was once used as a tool by farmers to call their cattle from the pastures and to communicate with other individuals. Although in the present day, it's no longer used for its original function, the alphorn has evolved into a tourist attraction and is symbolic of Switzerland.

Worldwide alphorn blowers gather to attend the Valais Drink Pure Alphorn Festival in Nendaz every July. On a mountain plateau above the village, the event presents a traditional costume parade, alphorn beginner courses, the official alphorn blowing contest, and phenomenal alphorn concerts performed by over 150 musicians simultaneously.

## 6. Swiss National Day

**Location:** Neuhausen am Rheinfall, Eastern Switzerland

**Months of Operation:** July 31st / August 1st

The Swiss National Day takes place annually on August 1st to celebrate the 1291 summer, when Uri, Schwyz, and Unterwalden, the three cantons, ended a historical alliance that is regarded as the Swiss Confederation's foundation.

National flags richly decorate buildings, bakers create special bread rolls, and children roam the nighttime streets holding lighted paper lanterns. Firework displays organized by the municipalities and several hilltop bonfires are the highlights of the celebrations.

A special celebration occurs at the Rhine Falls, close to Schaffhausen. Taking place a day early, Europe's most massive waterfalls are illuminated on July 31st with a phenomenal light display and spectacular fireworks show.

# 7. Schwägalp Schwinget

**Location:** Urnäsch, Eastern Switzerland

**Months of Operation:** Mid-August

A traditional Swiss sport closely resembling wrestling, Schwingen is a dueling match between two physically mighty combatants and features its own rules, throws, and grips. The nation's top wrestlers, the acclaimed "wicked ones," or Bösen, pit their physical prowess at various Schwingen festivals that usually occur in a remarkable natural setting.

One of these festivals in the Appenzell region is the Schwägalp Schwinget, situated just below the fearsome Säntis peak. This event amazes its spectators with the mighty force of nature and the impressive strength of the fighters.

# 8. Cattle Descent

**Location:** Charmey, Fribourg Region

**Months of Operation:** Late September

In multiple Swiss regions, late summer is a time of festivities. After spending over four months on the Alpine pastures, farmers and their animals adorned in lively decorations make a grand departure to the plains. However, rarely is this celebration showcased as exuberantly and boisterously as in Canton Freiburg's Charmey.

Like other cattle descents throughout Switzerland, the Désalpe de Charmey is incredible. Held annually in late September on the last Saturday, this celebration can't be beaten for individuals who value traditions.

The end of the alpine summer season is signaled by alpine roses, chrysanthemums, dahlias, and fir twigs towering in vibrant bunches on top of cows' heads. It's a grand day of importance for the alp's inhabitants, who call the mountain heights their home. They prepare early at sunrise for their triumphant entrance into the village after being away from home for four months.

They lead their cows, goats, sheep, and cattle back to the alpine barns early in the morning, preparing them for the procession. The procession starts to move subsequently. Proudly, the alpine farmers flaunt their traditional outfits and parade their livestock amongst the spectators. The lively festivities of the alpine homecomers are heard from vast distances. In the homeland of Gruyère AOP cheese, the homecoming group is celebrated and cheered on like heroes—alphorn blowers, yodelers, and flag wavers flaunt their skills on the village square to honor the homecoming group.

The Cattle Descent captivates a growing number of visitors annually, who wander around the great market with its regional specialties and products for arts and crafts.

## 9. Chestnut Festival

**Location:** Ascona, Ticino

**Months of Operation:** Mid-October

Once regarded as a poor man's food long ago, chestnuts are making a remarkable comeback to the Ticino region's kitchens. For centuries, Ticino considered the sweet chestnut the essential staple food, which still takes center stage at various festivals. In the modern day, the locals take pride in their culinary heritage, and chestnuts are served throughout the canton in multiple forms—such as traditionally roasted as chestnut gnocchi or marrons glacés.

In honor of this regional delicacy, the picturesque town of Ascona organizes a chestnut festival every October. With a musical entertainment spectacle, visitors are encouraged to savor over 2,000 kg of these fire-roasted fruits and many other chestnut-based delicacies, such as marmalade, fancy cakes, honey, and ice cream.

## 10. Zibelemärit

**Location:** Bern, Bern Region

**Months of Operation:** Late November

On the fourth Monday in November every year, the Swiss capital hosts the adored Zibelemärit. While the upper region of old town Bern, between the railway station and Bundesplatz, transforms into a grand marketplace, the air in the city streets fills with the sweet fragrance of Glühwein and onion tarts.

As the day continues, visitors in the thousands indulge in the delicious specialties and artistic braids of woven onion, which local farmers in hundreds of stalls sell, as well as a variety of drupes, nuts, and winter vegetables.

In addition, market vendors offer their regular merchandise for sale. Once school is out and the working day is over, the carnival spirit seizes the crowd in the afternoon and evening. These festivities include confetti matches, individuals in disguise, and small gatherings of people who dress up as jesters in restaurants who perform spin-offs of events that took place last year. During this time, satirical leaflets also show up in the streets.

The onion market, or Zibelemärit, is the last remaining feature of a fourteen-day autumn market that took place way back in the fifteenth century. A frequently told legend dates back to the 1405 city fire. The local farmers were granted the right to sell their products in the city after they assisted with the cleanup. However, 1439 was only when the first autumn market occurred, while farmers offered vegetables at the weekly markets for sale. Finally, in the middle of the nineteenth century, the first documented mention of onions appeared, as a railway line was being constructed connecting the farming lands into the city.

# 11. Fête de l'Escalade

**Location:** Geneva, Geneva

**Months of Operation:** December 11–12th

The Genevan festival celebrated annually in December, known as the Escalade, celebrated Geneva's 1602 victory against the Duke of Savoy's soldiers after they attacked the city during the night of December 11–12th. The Duke of Savoy, who had lost his former control of Geneva, fought to reclaim it. The battle was intense and violent, but the people of Geneva defended their town valiantly.

The event transports you to the 17th century as roughly 800 people parading in traditional costumes travel around Old Town Geneva on horseback or foot. Cozy up to a warm bonfire while indulging in marmite en chocolate, the classic chocolate cauldron, a tasty treat for chocoholics.

Many examples of bravery were born after the battle; one such hero is Mère Royaume, who scaled up to the ramparts and doused the head of a Savoyard soldier with her pot of hot soup.

Since this historic day, the citizens of Geneva have not forgotten and continue to celebrate their victorious day. A sizeable, torch-wielding march of people adorned in period costumes proceeds into the streets of the old city along each bank of the Rhone. Legendary historical figures are always present, like Mère Royaume armed with her famous pot. The procession pauses along the traditional route at multiple points, and a horseback herald recites the victory proclamation over the invaders. Then, arriving in jolly spirits, the participants sing patriotic tunes at St. Peter's Cathedral. Generalized merrymaking concludes the entire ceremony.

# First-Time Visit to Switzerland - What to Expect + Travel Tips

## Getting Around - Public Transportation

» Getting around Switzerland is hassle-free thanks to the country's extensive, impressively coordinated network of buses, trains, and boats. In addition, due to the plentiful cable bars, funiculars, and cog railways, mountaintops are adequately accessible.

» The SBB Mobile app is convenient for viewing timetables and using all public transportation methods to plan a route. Regardless of the way of travel, service is consistent, safe, and comfortable, with convenient connections.

## Swiss Travel Pass

» For complimentary travel on trains, buses, and boats throughout Switzerland, the Swiss Travel Pass is straightforward and fully comprehensive. Benefits of the pass include specific mountain excursions (and a half-off discount on several mountain railways not covered), trips on premier panoramic trains, public transportation in 90 urban regions, and entrance to over 500 museums.

» Various Swiss Travel Passes are available: for 3, 4, 8, or 15 successive days.

» Several websites and service desks at Swiss rail stations sell Swiss Travel Passes. Purchasing a pass in advance also saves time.

## Transportation by Train in Switzerland

» Several railway companies in Switzerland work together to create Switzerland's rail network. Swiss Federal Railways, the primary company, is referred to by its German initials SBB, French initials CFF, and Italian initials FFS.

» Board train and station announcements are made in the regional language. In addition, reports in English are available on long-distance trains waiting at main stations in popular tourist attractions.

» Although the trains are only sometimes 100% timely, they are consistently well-maintained. Thankfully, trains are frequent, so travel disruptions are minimal.

## Tickets + Reservations

» Train tickets are available for purchase at ticket counters or machines in railway stations, online, or through the SBB Mobile app. In addition, rail passes can be ordered online or at Swiss Railway stations.
» For the majority of trains in Switzerland, making reservations isn't essential. All you need to do is board the train with a rail pass and choose a vacant seat. However, international trains and trains on scenic routes, such as the Glacier Express and Bernina Express, are exceptions, as seat reservations with an additional fee are mandatory.

## First and Second-Class Seat Types

» First and second-class cars are available on Swiss trains. First-class cars are labeled with a 1 and yellow stripe on the car's exterior. Above the station platform, signs indicate the sector the cars will stop at (the front and rear of the train is usually where first class is located). Occasionally, a car will have first-

class and second-class seats in different sections.
» Most travelers choose second class, so they tend to be more crowded and noisy. However, besides first-class seats being slightly roomier, there is hardly any difference in comfort between the two.

## On-Board Services

» A restaurant serving appetizers, meals, and drinks is featured on InterCity and EuroCity trains. A few other trains offer a mini-bar/catering cat that goes around selling snacks and drinks.
» Certain trains, but not all, are equipped with electrical outlets.

## Travel by Bus in Switzerland

» Occasionally you can purchase tickets from a machine on board or a machine at a bus stop depending on the city you're in.

## Credit Cards, ATMs, and Currency

» The Swiss Franc (CHF) is the currency used in Switzerland.
» Credit card use is widely accepted for purchases in Switzerland.

> » ATMs are abundant in Switzerland. However, some are not connected to the interbank network known as Plus System.

## Expenses in Switzerland

> » Compared to other countries in Europe, Switzerland is on the pricier side. Paying for food, accommodations, transportation, and entertainment can make traveling on a tight budget difficult.
> » Expect a hefty bill when dining out in Switzerland. On average, main courses alone cost between 20 and 50 francs.
> » The price you'll pay for accommodations depends on the location and time of year. Generally, a good selection of 3 and 4-star hotels will cost $150–$300 CAD per night, but several cost over CAD 300 per night.

## Accommodations

> » Three and 4-star hotels in Switzerland are tidy and comfortable and have WIFI and tasty breakfast.
> » Hotel room sizes are similar to what you'd find in North America.
> » Certain hotels offer small washcloths, while others do not. Regardless, it's better to bring your supply, just in case.

## Safety

- » Switzerland is generally a very safe country, even for female solo travelers. Of all industrialized countries, it has one of the lowest crime rates, but theft can still happen, so it's best to keep personal belongings attended.

## Dining Out and Cuisine

- » Food in Switzerland is high quality, and finding enjoyable meals is easy, even for picky eaters.
- » There is regional variance between traditional cuisines, and it is most common to find dishes influenced by neighboring countries. Italian restaurants, for example, are widely popular.
- » As a standard European policy, water in restaurants must be paid for. Both still and sparkling bottled water are offered. In addition, you may also have to pay for tap water.
- » Since service is included in the meal price, there's no need to tip in Switzerland. However, rounding up your bill to the nearest whole number is a way to show gratitude for exceptional service.

» 12:00 p.m. to 2:00 p.m. is the typical time lunch is served, while dinner runs from 6:00 p.m. to 9:30 p.m. Compared to smaller towns, cities have more eateries that serve hot meals throughout the day (11:00 a.m. to 10:00 p.m.).

## Electricity

» 230 V is the voltage used in Switzerland.
» You can find multiple electrical sockets, and occasionally in a hotel room. Type J (3-pin) sockets are the most abundant, both recessed and flat. But types C and F (2-pin) are also available.

## Public Restrooms

» A mixture of paid public toilets and free ones are available.

## Walking and Hiking

» Switzerland has several well-maintained footpaths. Yellow signs waymark these paths, usually with an estimated time to the following destination.
» A red stripe on a white background indicates hiking routes on mountain paths. The waymark is usually displayed on the yellow signs but is occasionally painted on trees, rocks, and buildings.

## Cycling and Mountain Biking

» In Switzerland, bike routes are marked with red signposts signaling the distance to the following destination. Single-digit numbers indicate national passages. Double-digit numbers indicate regional roads, and triple-digit numbers indicate local routes.

» Cycling routes are usually on paved roads or paths but occasionally have unpaved sections. More natural surfaces and single tracks make up mountain bike routes.

» Most railway stations and rental shops offer bicycles (mountain, standard, and e-bikes), for rent. Rent-a-Bike has approximately 200 locations, 80 of which are located at railway stations. These bikes are of excellent quality and well-maintained.

» Most SBB trains, private railways, and Post Buses accept bicycles on board as long as a separate bike ticket or Day Bike Pass is purchased. Some boats also take bikes on board. In addition, bicycle-friendly train cars are marked on the door with a bike symbol. Unfortunately, Post Buses have limited bike space, and a few routes require a reservation. Alternatively, you can ship your bike as luggage from the train station, with a two-day delivery time.

# Miscellaneous Travel Information to Switzerland

» Safe drinking water is available in town squares at the public water fountains. To save money and limit waste, carry a refillable water bottle and fill it up at the water fountains.
» In specific destinations, a guest card is issued to anyone spending at least a night in the city or region. These cards provide free usage of local public transportation and frequent discounts on attractions.
» Many useful apps are available to people traveling to Switzerland. For example, SBB Mobile is excellent for transportation planning, you can navigate hiking and biking routes with Switzerland Mobility, and Swiss Travel Guide features attraction highlights.

# References

**Geography – Facts and Figures**

https://www.eda.admin.ch/aboutswitzerland/en/home/umwelt/geografie/geografie---fakten-und-zahlen.html

**Facts about the Swiss Alps**

https://www.alpenwild.com/staticpage/facts-about-the-swiss-alps/

**Facts about the Rhine River**

https://www.rolcruise.co.uk/blog/facts-about-the-rhine-river

**Rhône River Facts**

https://www.tauck.com/river-cruises/european-river-facts/rhone-river-facts

**Floating Down the River Reuss**

https://www.inyourpocket.com/lucerne/floating-down-the-river-reuss_155941v

**Reuss**

https://www.myswitzerland.com/en-us/destinations/reuss/

**River Ticino**

https://www.myswitzerland.com/en-
us/destinations/ticino-river/

**Swiss Plateau**

https://www.eda.admin.ch/aboutswitzerland/en/home
/umwelt/geografie/mittelland.html

**10 Most-Produced Agriculture Commodities in Switzerland**

https://scienceagri.com/10-most-produced-agriculture-
commodities-from-switzerland/

**Best Hikes Worldwide: Jura Crest Trail, Switzerland – Ali Rowsell**

https://www.wiredforadventure.com/jura-crest-trail-
switzerland/

**Hiking the Swiss Jura**

https://www.thecatandthepeacock.com/hiking-the-
swiss-jura

**Transportation Museum Lucerne**

https://swissfamilyfun.com/transportation-museum-
luzern/

**Swiss National Museum (Landesmuseum Zurich)**

https://travel.usnews.com/Zurich_Switzerland/Things
_To_Do/Swiss_National_Museum_23828/#:~:
text=The%20Swiss%20National%20Museum%
20is,and%20children%2016%20and%20younger

**Kunstmuseum Basel**

https://museums.eu/museum/details/742/kunstmuseum-basel

**The Olympic Museum**

https://www.myswitzerland.com/en-us/experiences/the-olympic-museum/

**Musée international de la Croix-Rouge et du Croissant-Rouge (MICR)**

https://www.myswitzerland.com/en-us/experiences/international-red-cross-museum/

**Cultural Life**

https://switzerland-tour.com/information/cultural-life

**Swiss Cuisine: Traditional Foods You Must Try – Valmira Rashiti**

https://studyinginswitzerland.com/swiss-cuisine-traditional-food-to-try/

**The 10 Best Restaurants in Switzerland – Elizabeth Heath**

https://www.tripsavvy.com/best-restaurants-in-switzerland-5211600

**Climate**

https://switzerland-tour.com/information/climate

**10 Great Outdoor Adventures in Switzerland**

https://www.hotels.com/go/switzerland/outdoor-adventures-switzerland

### Architecture

https://switzerland-tour.com/information/architecture

### 20 Famous Landmarks of Switzerland to Plan Your Travels Around!

https://inspiredbymaps.com/famous-landmarks-of-switzerland/

### Flora & Fauna

https://switzerland-tour.com/information/flora-fauna

### Honest Review: Aquatis Aquarium-Vivarium, Lausanne

https://www.touringswitzerland.com/honest-review-aquatis-aquarium-vivarium-lausanne/

### Natur- und Tierpark Goldau

https://en.wikipedia.org/wiki/Natur-_und_Tierpark_Goldau

### Top Traditional Events

https://www.myswitzerland.com/en-us/experiences/summer-autumn/listicles/top-traditional-events/

### What to Expect on Your First Trip to Switzerland - A First Time Visitor's Guide – Rhonda Krause

https://www.travelyesplease.com/what-to-expect-first-trip-to-switzerland/

## 11 Luxurious Hotels in Switzerland, From Fairy-tale Castles to Modern Chalets – Caitlin Morton

https://www.travelandleisure.com/hotels-to-book-in-switzerland-6835619

Printed in Great Britain
by Amazon